How to
Raise
Spiritually
Healthy Kids

PARENTING

Interactions Small Group Series

Authenticity: Being Honest with God and Others
Character: Reclaiming Six Endangered Qualities
Commitment: Developing Deeper Devotion to Christ
Community: Building Relationships within God's Family
Essential Christianity: Practical Steps for Spiritual Growth
Fruit of the Spirit: Living the Supernatural Life
Getting a Grip: Finding Balance in Your Daily Life
Jesus: Seeing Him More Clearly
Lessons on Love: Building Deeper Relationships
Living in God's Power: Finding God's Strength for Life's Challenges
Love in Action: Experiencing the Joy of Serving
Marriage: Building Real Intimacy
Meeting God: Psalms for the Highs and Lows of Life
New Identity: Discovering Who You Are in Christ
Parenting: How to Raise Spiritually Healthy Kids
Prayer: Opening Your Heart to God
Reaching Out: Sharing God's Love Naturally
The Real Deal: Discover the Rewards of Authentic Relationships
Significance: Understanding God's Purpose for Your Life
Transformation: Letting God Change You from the Inside Out

InterActions
small group series

How to
Raise
Spiritually
Healthy Kids

PARENTING

Previously published as *Parenthood*

BILL HYBELS

WITH KEVIN AND SHERRY HARNEY

ZONDERVAN™

GRAND RAPIDS, MICHIGAN 49530 USA

WILLOW
Willow Creek Resources

ZONDERVAN™

Parenting
Copyright © 1996 by Willow Creek Association
Previously published as *Parenthood*

Requests for information should be addressed to:

Zondervan, *Grand Rapids, Michigan 49530*

ISBN-10: 0-310-26590-8
ISBN-13: 978-0-310-26590-0

Interior design by Rick Devon and Michelle Espinoza

Printed in the United States of America

05 06 07 08 09 10 11 12 /❖ DCI/ 10 9 8 7 6 5 4 3 2 1

CONTENTS

Interactions 7

Introduction: How to Raise
    Spiritually Healthy Kids 9

SESSION 1
    To Be or Not to Be? 11

SESSION 2
    Raising Whole Children 19

SESSION 3
    Affirming Each Child's Uniqueness . . 27

SESSION 4
    Mistakes Parents Make 33

SESSION 5
    The Home as Trauma Center. 39

SESSION 6
    Teaching Faith in the Home 47

Leader's Notes 53

INTERACTIONS

In 1992, Willow Creek Community Church, in partnership with Zondervan and the Willow Creek Association, released a curriculum for small groups entitled the Walking with God series. In just three years, almost a half million copies of these small group study guides were being used in churches around the world. The phenomenal response to this curriculum affirmed the need for relevant and biblical small group materials.

At the writing of this curriculum, there are nearly 3,000 small groups meeting regularly within the structure of Willow Creek Community Church. We believe this number will increase as we continue to place a central value on small groups. Many other churches throughout the world are growing in their commitment to small group ministries as well, so the need for resources is increasing.

In response to this great need, the Interactions small group series has been developed. Willow Creek Association and Zondervan have joined together to create a whole new approach to small group materials. These discussion guides are meant to challenge group members to a deeper level of sharing, to create lines of accountability, to move followers of Christ into action, and to help group members become fully devoted followers of Christ.

SUGGESTIONS FOR INDIVIDUAL STUDY

1. Begin each session with prayer. Ask God to help you understand the passage and to apply it to your life.
2. A good modern translation, such as the New International Version, the New American Standard Bible, or the New Revised Standard Version, will give you the most help. Questions in this guide are based on the New International Version.
3. Read and reread the passage(s). You must know what the passage says before you can understand what it means and how it applies to you.
4. Write your answers in the spaces provided in the study guide. This will help you to express clearly your understanding of the passage.
5. Keep a Bible dictionary handy. Use it to look up unfamiliar words, names, or places.

SUGGESTIONS FOR GROUP STUDY

1. Come to the session prepared. Careful preparation will greatly enrich your time in group discussion.
2. Be willing to join in the discussion. The leader of the group will not be lecturing, but will encourage people to discuss what they have learned in the passage. Plan to share what God has taught you in your individual study.
3. Stick to the passage being studied. Base your answers on the verses being discussed rather than on outside authorities such as commentaries or your favorite author or speaker.
4. Try to be sensitive to the other members of the group. Listen attentively when they speak, and be affirming whenever you can. This will encourage more hesitant members of the group to participate.
5. Be careful not to dominate the discussion. By all means participate! But allow others to have equal time.
6. If you are the discussion leader, you will find additional suggestions and helpful ideas in the leader's notes.

ADDITIONAL RESOURCES AND TEACHING MATERIALS

At the end of this study guide you will find a collection of resources and teaching materials to help you in your growth as a follower of Christ. You will also find resources that will help your church develop and build fully devoted followers of Christ.

INTRODUCTION: HOW TO RAISE SPIRITUALLY HEALTHY KIDS

The scene is a rustic Rocky Mountain cabin. The group is all male. Most of us are leaders of corporations or Christian ministries. The question posed to us is, "How did you feel about your parents when you were growing up?" What followed was a session that I'll never forget. It was an emotionally-charged evening.

One guy said, "My dad was my hero. Not only was he a model and a mentor to me, he was a confidant and my best friend."

Another guy looked at the floor and with a carefully-restrained voice said, "My dad was an inconsistent, anger-filled alcoholic who made every day of my life a living nightmare. I hated him every day of my life. And the more I realize what he did to my mother and my brothers and sisters, the more I detest the man now. My father was a disaster."

"My mother deserves a purple heart," one older guy said proudly. "She raised four boys during the depression. She worked nights—every night. And yet she still found time to make sure we had school lunches, clean clothes, and warm beds. How she did it, we'll never know. We call her a saint. She was the godliest, most selfless person I knew. They don't make them like my mom anymore."

Later one of the young men in the group said, "Now that I think about it, my mother was sort of a non-person. To this day, I don't know how she took the degradation she received from my father. She never stood up to him. She never staked out her own territory. She never expressed a contrary view. She just existed. I never really knew who she was."

On and on these men talked about their parents, late into the night. What I noticed was that every time a guy made a comment about his parents, it was packed with emotion. Say what you will about the subject of family, one thing is sure, few subjects touch us as deeply as family matters.

In this small group study guide we will come face to face with the issues that matter most to us: how to decide if you should have children, learning to raise whole and healthy children, affirming each child's unique qualities, dealing with the mistakes parents make, the home as a healing center, and teaching faith in the home. Although these may be emotionally-packed topics, they are critical if we are going to be the kind of parents God longs for us to be.

Some people come to a study like this with eager anticipation about what they are going to learn. Others might be frantically searching for ways to cope with the trauma that this subject matter evokes in them. You might live with the trauma of having been raised in a home that didn't work very well. You may be dealing with trauma from twisted family dynamics that have left deep wounds and scars. With God's help, this series of interactions can be a tool for learning, and also part of the healing process for you.

Bill Hybels

TO BE OR NOT TO BE?

THE BIG PICTURE

"When are you going to start having children?" That's the question so many couples hear after they get married. Friends and family members sometimes even ask this question *before* the couple is married. It seems marriage and children just go together. Many people approach this topic with a built-in presupposition that all those who get married are expected and obligated to have children.

In recent years I have begun to struggle with this presupposition. I have started to wonder if every married couple *ought* to have children. In the past I have even spoken on this topic and have written down some of my personal feelings about the idea that all married couples ought to move naturally toward having a family.

I found out firsthand how controversial this subject is after the release of a book I wrote entitled *Honest To God?*. Buried in a remote part of chapter seven, I just happened to mention that maybe, because of the times we live in, it might be time for married couples to think twice before starting a family. Maybe it's time to submit a decision of that magnitude to careful prayer and thorough analysis before making plans to get pregnant two years after the wedding. I even went so far as to suggest that maybe, just maybe, there are valid reasons for holding off on having children for a time. And quite possibly there are some valid reasons why God would lead some couples to decide not to have children at all.

Little did I know how many people would be upset by that notion. Letters of protest began coming in. As I read the reasoning behind some of those protests, I found myself more motivated than ever to go on record as saying that *parenthood might not be for everybody*. I also found myself moved to clearly state that bringing children into today's world is a decision that had better involve a lot of sincere prayer and sober-mindedness.

A WIDE ANGLE VIEW

1 Respond to these statements:

There are some couples who should never have children.

We live in a day when serious prayer and reflection should precede any couple's decision to have children.

Marriage is about family. If a couple gets married, they should plan to have children. That's God's design for marriages.

A BIBLICAL PORTRAIT

Read Colossians 3:18–21

2 In this passage we find words of challenge to family members. Take a moment and put each challenge in your own words.

v. 18—Wives . . .

v. 19—Husbands . . .

v. 20—Children . . .

v. 21—Fathers (Parents) . . .

What kind of a spirit would begin to develop in a family who followed these biblical challenges?

3 Why are mutual submission and mutual love essential between a husband and wife who are seeking to raise healthy children?

What leads to, and what can hinder, mutual submission and mutual love?

SHARPENING THE FOCUS

Read Snapshot "Times Have Changed"

TIMES HAVE CHANGED

The world in which we raise children today is dramatically different than it was just one or two decades ago. In the 1960s we sang "I want to hold your hand." Today fifth graders sing "I want your sex." When I was a kid, Eddie Haskell on "Leave It to Beaver" was the rowdiest kid on television. My mother would pull me aside and say, "Don't ever hang around with guys like Eddie Haskell. They'll mess up your life." Today you flip through the channels and are bombarded with programs sensationalizing rape, incest, homosexuality, and satanic-inspired ritual murders. Times have changed.

13

4 What changes have you seen in the world since you were a child in the following areas?

- The media (music, TV, and movies)

- Views of sexuality

- Respect for authority

- Substance abuse

- The importance of the family

5 How do these changes impact children growing up today?

What personal fears or concerns do you experience as you think of raising your own children?

Read Snapshot "Wounded Parents"

WOUNDED PARENTS

Parents these days tend to be more wounded themselves than they were a generation ago. Surveys of married couples between the ages of twenty and thirty-five reveal that alarming numbers of these husbands and wives have come from divorced families, troubled families, and dysfunctional homes, or were brought up by alcohol or drug abusers. Record numbers of husbands and wives have been physically, emotionally, or sexually abused. As you might expect, these traumas tend to cause deep wounds in the lives of husbands and wives. If those wounds are not treated carefully and not processed thoroughly, they often end up infecting and poisoning the marriage relationship. And if children are already on the scene, inevitably the toxicity of the parents' wounds affects their lives as well.

6 How were you wounded in your upbringing, and how could this experience impact your ability to effectively parent?

What steps have you taken to seek healing in this area of woundedness?

What work remains to be done as you move forward?

Read Snapshot "Three Critical Questions"

THREE CRITICAL QUESTIONS

Because of the climate of our culture and world, we need to be prayerful and wise about having children. Also, because many adults are still deeply wounded, we need to slow down and be discerning before we jump into family life. To help in this process of evaluation and discernment, reflect on the following three questions:

1. What are you doing to build your marriage so that it will last a lifetime?

2. What have you done to work through areas of your brokenness?

3. How would you gauge your level of commitment to paying the price of raising children?

Once you have prayerfully and honestly answered these questions you can look at parenting with a healthy and responsible perspective.

7 Take time alone with your spouse to discuss the three critical questions in the above Snapshot. Then come back to the group and reflect on the additional questions below.

What costs are involved in raising children in this day and age?

What sacrifices are you going to have to make if you want to raise healthy children?

Read Snapshot "Passing a Broken Baton?"

PASSING A BROKEN BATON?

In previous generations couples could get married and for the most part assume that their partner would be emotionally healthy. Not so today. Those days are probably gone forever. The moral, spiritual, and relational disintegration occurring in our culture over the last twenty or thirty years has generated record numbers of young married couples from broken and troubled homes and drug- and alcohol-tainted environments.

These same couples are all fired up about having children without first paying the price to process the pain, anger, and disappointment of the wounds they received in their families of origin. As a result, this "brokenness" gets passed from generation to the next like a baton in a relay race. Generation after generation receives the same broken baton. It's time to break this cycle of brokenness.

8 As a result of this session, discuss the changes you would like to make in order to bring wholeness to your life and marriage. Find a partner in the group. Share your thoughts and pray for one another.

PUTTING YOURSELF IN THE PICTURE

SEEKING WHOLENESS

If you identified an experience in your childhood where you were wounded, what will you do in the coming month to seek healing in this area of your life? Who are the people who will support you in this process? What are the resources available to help you? If you are not sure what steps to take as you move toward healing and wholeness, seek the counsel of a mature Christian relative, friend, pastor, or a Christian counselor.

A LIFETIME COMMITMENT

If we are going to raise whole and healthy children, a solid marriage commitment is an essential asset. Take time in the coming week to reaffirm your commitment to your spouse "as long as you both shall live!" Review your wedding vows and discuss how you are doing at keeping them. If you have an audio or video tape of your wedding ceremony, take time to watch it together and discuss how you can continue to grow more in love with each other.

RAISING WHOLE CHILDREN

REFLECTIONS FROM SESSION 1

1. If you identified an area from your childhood where you need to seek healing, how have you begun the process of seeking healing? If you have sensed God's healing hand in your heart and life, tell your group members about your experience.
2. If you took time since the last small group to reaffirm your marriage vows, how did you do this? What difference has this reaffirmation made in your relationship with your spouse?

THE BIG PICTURE

You know, it might just be me, but it seems like every time I turn around I'm hearing or reading about another breakthrough in the field of genetics. Scientists seem to be chomping at the bit to learn how to custom design kids through genetic engineering. Sometimes I wonder where all of that is headed. Can you imagine twenty years from now getting a "Kids-R-Us" catalog in the mail? A four-color, slick promotional piece with models and descriptions of kids so that people could order exactly the kind of child they wanted. It sounds a little far fetched, doesn't it? But I do wonder how many people would jump at the chance to design their "perfect" child.

I wonder if we're not working on the wrong side of the equation. Maybe if we're concerned about the children of future generations, we ought to focus our attention on redesigning or reengineering *parents*. Maybe we should reengineer parents to be able to raise whatever child God gives them to become a whole child. What if we had a "Parents-R-Us" catalog, with page after page containing descriptions of special abilities that parents could bring to bear on the children God puts in their care? That sounds like the better route to go.

A WIDE ANGLE VIEW

1 If you could custom design the "perfect" child, what three or four characteristics would be most important. Why did you choose those characteristics?

If you could custom design the "perfect" parent, what three or four characteristics would be most important. Why did you choose those characteristics?

A BIBLICAL PORTRAIT

Read Deuteronomy 6:4–9

2 In verse four of this passage we are reminded that there is one true God. In the fifth verse we are called to, "Love the LORD your God with all your heart and with all your soul and with all your strength." What does it mean to love God with:

- All your heart

- All your soul

- All your strength

How does someone rekindle their love for God?

3 In verses six through nine we are given specific instructions on how we should raise children. What are these instructions, and why are they so important?

If our goal is to raise whole and healthy children, why is the truth of this passage essential?

SHARPENING THE FOCUS

Read Snapshot "Building Self-Esteem"

BUILDING SELF-ESTEEM

Building a strong self-esteem into your children is vitally important. There's been so much printed and said about self-esteem in the last twenty years that I fear many parents believe it has become just another buzzword—that it's just psychological mumbo jumbo that doesn't amount to much in the long run. But nothing could be further from the truth. One of the most important contributions you can make to your children is to convince them that they really matter—to God, to you, and to other people. They need to know they're unique and important; they're valuable and irreplaceable; and they're worthy of respect. Children need to be told they are worthy of being loved and treasured. They must know that their thoughts, feelings, doubts, and fears are important and worthy of careful discussion. This kind of healthy self-esteem sets a foundation for a healthy life.

---

4 As a parent, how do you sometimes tear down the self-esteem of your children?

How can you be more intentional about building up the self-esteem of your children with:

- A word

- A look

- A touch

Read Snapshot "Developing a Sense of Personal Competence"

DEVELOPING A SENSE OF PERSONAL COMPETENCE

Another challenge in raising whole children is to develop a sense of personal competence. As you have just discussed, it is essential that children know they are worth something. It is equally important for them to develop a sense that they can do some things well. Self-esteem has to do with value; a sense of competence has to do more with performance and ability. I get very concerned when I hear parents say, in effect, "Our adorable little Andrew is the greatest gift in our lives, and we tell him that all the time. He's nine, and he can't read or write very well, and he's flunking out of school, but we keep assuring him that he is our little treasure no matter how he performs in school." When I hear that, I say to myself, "Little Andrew might have high self-esteem, but he's going to find out in the not-too-distant future that a good self-image is not going to deliver a diploma on a silver platter. A good self-image alone is not going to secure him acceptance into college or a challenging position in the marketplace. A healthy self-image doesn't pay the rent."

Somewhere alone the line, parents have to integrate the understanding of the importance of competence in the lives of their children. Somewhere along the way, parents are going to have to explain to their children that the real world demands a certain level of expertise and certain skills in order for wages to be earned and food bills to be paid. And that competence training should start early on.

5 In what areas of life did your parents help you develop personal competence?

What can you do to help your children develop a sense of personal competence? Choose one of the following areas and express your thoughts to the group:

- Academically
- Athletically
- Conversationally
- Mechanically
- Domestically
- Musically
- Artistically
- Recreationally

Read Snapshot "Developing Relational Skills"

DEVELOPING RELATIONAL SKILLS

Another challenge in raising whole children is to teach them relational skills. In the last thirty years, we've witnessed breathtaking advances in research, technology, and manufacturing. We've gotten better at building computers, cars, missiles, and microchips. But ironically, in that same era, we've grown steadily worse in our ability to build and sustain human relationships.

Fragmented families, chaotic home environments, television, VCRs, and video games are all combining to produce a generation of relationally-inept children. Children who can't discern how they're really feeling inside, much less communicate those feelings to someone else. Many children are incapable of expressing positive and negative emotions constructively. Other children don't have any idea what to do when an important relationship breaks down. In short, we're raising a whole generation of young people who really don't have a clue how healthy relationships function.

6 What are one or two good questions that could be "discussion starters" between you and your child? Be sure these questions will help them communicate their feelings clearly.

- Questions for a toddler

- Questions for a third grader

- Questions for a junior high student

- Questions for a senior high student

7 What were some of the things the adults in your life did when you were growing up that helped you develop healthy relational skills?

What are some of the things you can do to help the children in your life become more effective in how they relate with others?

Read Snapshot "The Spiritual Dimension of Life"

THE SPIRITUAL DIMENSION OF LIFE

 If you want to raise whole children, you cannot ignore the spiritual dimension of life. Today's parents like to pride themselves for being open-minded. They like to announce to their colleagues, "We're not going to indoctrinate our children religiously. And we're not going to bias the minds of our off-spring by giving them any religious training. We're going to allow our children to come to their own spiritual conclusions without any parental prejudice." That kind of philosophy sounds so modern and enlightened. But it is a fatally flawed way to approach raising children.

The flaw is in thinking that it's possible for a kid to grow up in a value-free environment. It's not true. Your son turns on the television set and receives thousands of value-intensive images that communicate values about morality, sexuality, ethics, money, power, pleasure, love, and hate. Your daughter plays with the neighbor kids and they tell her what they think is right and wrong. And in school kids are taught evolution, relativism, and safe sex habits. The fact is, there's no such thing as a value-free environment.

The real issue boils down to one simple question: Who is going to instill values into your children? Who's going to answer questions like, "Where did I come from?" and "Where am I going when I die?" and "How do we decide what is right and wrong?" Who's going to answer the tough questions like, "What is life really about? Is there a God who cares about me? What's the purpose of it all?"

---

8 How would you feel if your children's faith looked just like yours?

9

In seeking to be a positive role model for the children in your life, what areas deserve more attention so that you can deepen *your* personal spiritual life?

Ask group members to pray for you and keep you accountable as you seek to change.

PUTTING YOURSELF IN THE PICTURE

BUILDING COMPETENCY

If you already have a child or children, what is one area in which you want to help your child grow more competent? What will you do in the coming month to work with them in this area and help them grow in their own abilities and confidence?

If you don't have any children at this time, what is one area in which you want to develop a deeper level of personal competency? As you develop this, how can you impart some of what you are learning to a young person you know?

GROWING IN FAITH

As you take your own spiritual inventory, what area requires greater focus and depth? Set a personal growth goal for the coming month in this area. Consider personal Bible study, your prayer life, consistency in attending worship, journaling, and personal reflection. What will you do to grow in this area, and who will offer prayer support for you?

AFFIRMING EACH CHILD'S UNIQUENESS

REFLECTIONS FROM SESSION 2

1. If you have been working with a child to help them become more competent in an area, tell the group about your experience. What impact has this had on their self-esteem and on your relationship with them?
2. If you made a commitment to grow in an area of your spiritual life, how are you doing at keeping your commitment? What growth have you seen in your spiritual life?

THE BIG PICTURE

You have seen this scenario, and so have I. Three children are born and raised by the same parents in the same home. They attend the same church, the same school, and play in the same neighborhood. The parents break their backs to apply love and discipline consistently. They want to make sure they show no partiality to any one of the three children. And what often happens? Two of the three kids flourish. Two of them do well in school. Two of them have healthy relationships with families and friends. Two of the three grow up with a well-adjusted frame of mind, fall in love, get married, start families, and live happily ever after. But one child seems to turn the family upside down and inside out. That child raises the tension level in the home more than the other two children combined. That child pushes the parents to the absolute limits and sometimes beyond. School doesn't go well for that child. Friendships don't work well and life doesn't turn out well. And the rest of the family, especially the parents, scratch their heads and say, "How can it be? We did everything in our power to treat all the children exactly the same. Two of them flourish and one flounders. How can it be?"

The flip side of the scenario can be equally baffling. Three children grow up in a troubled home. The father drinks too much and works too hard. The mother is depressed and sullen most of the time. Very little affection flows in the family and there is almost no communication. By definition, the family is dysfunctional. It remains dysfunctional for the whole time the three kids are growing up. This family is destined to destroy the kids in equal measure. And sure enough, two of the three suffer all the negative consequences you would anticipate. But amazingly, one child survives. And doesn't just survive but mysteriously develops a depth of character and fortitude that serves her well throughout the course of her life. She flourishes. How can that be? Three children raised in an equally dreadful environment, but the result is anything but equal.

A WIDE ANGLE VIEW

1 How have you seen one of the above scenarios played out in life?

A BIBLICAL PORTRAIT

Read Psalm 139:1–18

2 This psalm tells us a great deal about God and ourselves. After reading it closely, take time as a group to do the following things:

- Write down how God feels about you.

- Tell other group members what you learn of God's character and work from this psalm.

3 Verses thirteen and fourteen talk about how God has made us. How are you fearfully and wonderfully made in the following areas?

- Physically

- Intellectually

- Emotionally

- Spiritually

- Temperamentally

As you think of your children, how are they wonderfully made?

SHARPENING THE FOCUS

Read Snapshot "Affirming Each Child's Unique Temperament"

AFFIRMING EACH CHILD'S UNIQUE TEMPERAMENT

We have all heard the theory that all kids are alike. They're merely shapeless blobs of flesh, devoid of any inherent properties. Identical lumps of clay that parents can shape into any form they wish because there are no innate characteristics or bents begging to be expressed.

Today child development experts are admitting to one another that these little lumps of flesh have wills of their own. Characters of their own. Bents of their own. Some of these little innocent tissue masses come into the world with a smile on their face and an olive branch in their mouth. "Just say the word, I'll do it!" Others come roaring onto the scene with a smirk on their face and a cigarette in their mouth. Some of them come with a look in their eye that says, "I'm going to push you to the limit every single day for the first seven years of my life. It's going to be ugly. Just try to get me to stay on line. Go ahead. Make my day!"

4

Circle the one statement in each line that most applies to you:

or

- I am more laid back than most people   I am more high strung than most people

- I tend to play it safe   I tend to take risks

- I communicate my feelings easily   I tend to keep my feelings to myself

- I like to plan things well in advance   I like to take things as they come along

- I like to figure things out on my own   I like to have clear directions for a project

As you think of your temperament and make-up, in what ways were you affirmed for these qualities as you grew up?

5

Why is it critically important for parents to affirm the temperament of each child?

What happens when you affirm your child's temperament?

Read Snapshot "Affirming Interests and Abilities"

AFFIRMING INTERESTS AND ABILITIES

I know career decisions are exceedingly complex. I know that the real world doesn't always offer a panacea of opportunity and remuneration for all of our yearnings and passions. I also know God has a way of arranging our circuitry so that most of us love something. Most of us are fascinated with a certain kind of endeavor. Most of us are fired up about a certain kind of concern. Those passions and motivated interests must be identified and taken into consideration if we're going to flourish and be fulfilled with our lives, our vocations and callings. Effective parenting demands that very early in the childrearing process, we begin to expose our children to a wide range of opportunities. Then we need to observe their reactions, likes, dislikes, successes, and failures. And when we begin to identify what really turns their crank, we need to talk to them about it. As their God-given interest and abilities surface, we need to affirm them and encourage them to develop in these areas.

6 What are some of the interests and abilities you see developing in your children?

What can you do to affirm and support them as they develop in these areas?

Read Snapshot "The Language of Love"

THE LANGUAGE OF LOVE

Every person has his or her style or preference when it comes to the giving and receiving of love. Parents need to affirm and cooperate with each child's uniqueness in their love language. One person says, "I'm a hugger. And when I feel love for a person, I automatically walk toward them with my arms out. I'm just going to attack them with an embrace. I can't help it. I love them. I'm a hugger." Another person says, "When I feel love, I just have to say it. I tell it to them verbally." Others communicate love by giving thoughtful gifts. They see something nice and say, "Oh, I've got to buy that for so-and-so. She will love it." Others show people that they're loved by acts of service. They show it by helping, supporting, and serving others. Others like to provide exciting opportunities for people they love. They arrange a meaningful experience for someone and say, "I did this for you because I knew that you'd love it, and I love you." And still others commit large time blocks just to be with the person they love. Identify the language of love each of your children speaks and then communicate with them often!

7
What most communicated love to you as a child?

What most communicates love to you now?

What do you think most communicates rlove to your children?

8
How can you speak the language of love more clearly to your children?

PUTTING YOURSELF IN THE PICTURE

DISCOVERING INTERESTS AND DESIRES

Take time in the coming week to do a one-on-one interview with each of your children. Use the questions below, as well as any of your own questions, to help you discover the desires and interests of your children.

- What things do you really enjoy doing?
- If you could pick anything and be sure you would not fail, what would you want to do?
- If you could do any job, what occupation would you choose?

After talking about these questions, ask each child what you can do as a parent to help them pursue the things they would really like to do with their life.

LANGUAGE LESSONS

In the coming month speak the language of love with each of your children. Be intentional about speaking three different ways with each child: through showing affection, through verbal affirmations of your love, and through a special gift of some kind. Watch their responses and try to discover what speaks the language of love most clearly to each one of them.

MISTAKES PARENTS MAKE

REFLECTIONS FROM SESSION 3

1. If you did an interview with one of your children, tell the group what you learned.
2. What have you discovered about the language of love each of your children speaks? What will you be doing to "speak" love clearly to each of your children?

THE BIG PICTURE

If you ever want to liven up a dull party, ask people in the group to recall and share an embarrassing mistake they made sometime in the past. I did this in a group of ministers once. I figure if it can work in a group of ministers, it can probably work anywhere!

One minister told about a time he was delayed at an airport and was very late to perform a wedding. He said he drove like a madman to the church and dashed into his office to get his Bible and wedding notes. He could hear the processional being played on the organ as he ran up the back steps of the altar area. He arrived at the platform at the precise moment the father was prepared to hand his daughter over to the groom.

All of a sudden he realized he didn't know the names of the couple he was about to marry. Someone else had done the rehearsal and counseling with this couple because he had been out of town. He didn't have a clue who these two people were and how he was going to refer to them during the ceremony. He was standing in front of a packed church and two starry-eyed lovers with no names.

When it came time for the vows, he simply said to the woman, "Now do you take this man to be your lawful wedded husband?" "I do." "And do you take this woman to be your lawful wedded wife." "I do." And things kept going. At the end of the ceremony the pastor was suppose to say, "Ladies and gentlemen, I present to you Mr. and Mrs. so-and-so." Instead, he turned up the drama another notch and at the end he said, "Ladies and gentlemen, God on this day has made this man a husband and has made this woman his bride. And I present them as husband and wife to all of you." The organ played, the people applauded, the bride and groom went down and hugged the parents and then went out to the reception line. And you guessed it, not a single person even realized that he had performed the whole wedding ceremony without mentioning the bride and groom's names one time.

A WIDE ANGLE VIEW

1
Describe in full color an embarrassing mistake you have made.

How do you respond to mistakes your kids make?

A BIBLICAL PORTRAIT

Read Proverbs 13:24 and 22:15

2
How does consistent and appropriate discipline show love?

3

How can loving discipline help a child grow in wisdom and maturity?

Think about an experience in your childhood when one of your parents disciplined you in an appropriate way. How did their discipline help you walk away from foolishness and toward wisdom?

SHARPENING THE FOCUS

Read Snapshot "Dealing with Discipline"

DEALING WITH DISCIPLINE

I can't count the number of times I've heard parents say in their later years of life, "I was way too hard on my kids. I was like a drill sergeant. I realize now that my children lived in terror. I administered discipline with a militaristic legalism. I was too firm. My kids were fearful of making a mistake because they knew the consequences were going to be swift and severe." When I hear these stories I sense regret and sadness in the voices of these parents.

An equal number of parents have regrets on the other side of the discipline equation. Some parents say, "I let my kids get away with highway robbery. I never drew lines or set limits or confronted attitude problems. I never made my kids face the consequences of their actions and now they're paying for my mistake. I failed to give loving and consistent discipline. They're irresponsible young people now who are headed for big trouble later on in life." They are also sad when they look back on how they failed to discipline their children.

4

What are some of the consequences of discipline that is administered with too heavy of a hand and not enough love?

What are some of the consequences when a parent fails to draw any lines, set any boundaries, or administer any discipline?

5 Allow various group members to tell a brief story of a child's misbehavior that led to some kind of discipline (but don't tell how they were disciplined). Have one or two group members tell how they would have handled disciplining the child if it was their responsibility to do so.

Read Snapshot "Expressing Emotions"

EXPRESSING EMOTIONS

Many parents feel the sting of remorse over how emotions were handled in the home. They failed to affirm the fact that feelings matter. They did not let their children express feelings freely. They did not understand the extent of the damage done to a child when his or her feelings are ignored, ridiculed, suppressed, or overpowered.

Parents need to learn that being sad is not necessarily bad. It's a valid emotion. It's a legitimate feeling. Children's sad feelings must be authenticated, not outlawed. When sad feelings are trivialized or labeled inappropriate or shamed, a child emotionally experiences the equivalent of a short-circuit.

The same thing happens when other emotions are mishandled by parents. When anger is outlawed or when excitement is diminished or when fear is not acknowledged, children are cheated of a chance to learn how to express emotions honestly.

---

6 Relate an example of a way emotions were typically expressed in the home where you grew up.

What are you doing to create a climate where feelings can be openly expressed by your children?

7

What are the possible consequences of a parent making the following statements to their child?

- "What are you crying about? Don't be such a baby!"

- "If you don't stop that crying, I'll give you something to cry about!"

- "Settle down and don't be so excited about things. You act so silly when you're excited."

- "You're such a big girl now, you can't still be scared of the dark. Grow up!"

- "You control your anger. Just learn to keep those feelings inside."

- "Don't be afraid to try that. Anyone can do it."

What are some positive and affirming statements you can say to your children when they experience the following feelings?

- Sadness

- Excitement

- Anger

- Fear

- Anxiety

Read Snapshot "Building Character"

BUILDING CHARACTER

Sometimes I worry that this generation is going to raise children who have little character because their parents have overprovided for them and overprotected them. I worry that we shelter our kids from the very experiences that helped make some of us strong. Maybe they need to learn to go without some things and even hear their parents say, "I can't afford that. We don't have the resources to have that experience." It might be good for them to have a paper route that forces them to get up before the sun rises five or six days a week. It might build character if they had to do some baby-sitting jobs to help pay for the needs of life and not just the wants and the extras. Mowing lawns, earning their own money, doing chores, riding bikes instead of being driven everywhere, applying for their own jobs, and not having parents who always give them the easy path could be exactly what our children need. What if they have to get a job that pays minimum wage or are asked to save some of their own money for college? Would this hurt our kids, or would it build character?

8

What did your parents do to develop and build character into your life through:

- Experiences they gave you

- Their own example

- Things they made you do

What are you doing to build character into the lives of your children through:

- Experiences you are giving them

- Your example

- Things you make them do

PUTTING YOURSELF IN THE PICTURE

SAYING "I'M SORRY!"

If you discipline too harshly or if you haven't disciplined enough, you need to say two powerful words: "I'm sorry." You may need to tell your child, "I'm sorry that you lived in terror" or "I'm sorry I let you get away with highway robbery and didn't draw lines and limits for you." Those two powerful words can change the whole nature of your relationship with your children. If that's appropriate and necessary for you, I want to encourage you to take the steps necessary to do this. You will be amazed what bridges can be built by saying those two words.

ADVENTURES IN CHARACTER BUILDING

What is one characteristic in your children that you desire to see strengthened? What can you do to help develop this quality in their lives? Helping them might mean challenging them to do some things on their own. It might mean taking away something that is hurting them. It might mean an investment of your time in their lives. Set a goal to invest in the life of a child. Find a friend who can pray for you and support you in this commitment.

THE HOME AS TRAUMA CENTER

REFLECTIONS FROM SESSION 4

1. If you took time to say, "I'm sorry" to one of your children, how did they respond? How did it feel to admit to your child that you were wrong? What did you learn from this experience?
2. If you made an effort to begin building character into the life of one of your children, what specific actions have you taken? How has this affected your child and your relationship?

THE BIG PICTURE

Most of us are not consciously aware of all the medical centers and trauma centers we pass as we drive along the road each day. But I suspect that all of us, when we see those trauma center signs along the highways, breathe a short sigh of relief. It's good to know that if any medical emergency should arise, there is a facility in the community that has a trained staff ready to meet our physical needs any time of the day or night. It's comforting to know that there is somewhere to go in case of a medical emergency.

Where do we go when we have a non-medical emergency? Where do we go for the emotional, psychological, and relational calamities of life? Where do we turn when our confidence collapses? When our self-esteem takes a beating? When our minds get all muddled up? When our spirits sag? When our feelings get hurt? When our hearts get broken? Wouldn't it be wonderful to have access to a trauma center for those kinds of injuries?

I believe with all my heart that our homes are meant to act as a trauma center in the midst of a harsh world. Our children should know that they have a safe haven in our homes. Home should be a harbor where they can set anchor in the midst of the storms of life and get the supplies they need to continue on the journey.

This hit home for me some years ago through an experience I had with my son, Todd. As we sat down for dinner, he was rather quiet. I noticed he seemed very reflective, but I didn't pursue it at the table. After supper, he played by himself until bedtime. When I was tucking him in and saying his prayers with him, I thought I would take a shot and see if I could get the little guy to talk to me about what was bothering him. I just said, "You seem kind of quiet tonight, pal. Anything you want to talk to your dad about?" He said, "No, Dad. Nothing." I said, "Are you really sure because I'm not going to bug you about it, but if you want to talk, you know I will lay down here with you and listen." He said, "No, I don't really want to say anything, but you can lay down by me." So I did. I just laid down with him awhile and silently prayed for wisdom.

After a few minutes of silence, without any prompting, Todd turned to me and said, "Dad, today a big kid on the bus called me weird." And then he burst out crying. He reached over for me to embrace him and I did. I hung onto him tightly for quite a time.

When he finally relaxed his hold on my neck, I started to administer a little fatherly CPR on his faltering heart. I told him how big kids sometimes say things because it makes them feel macho and tough. Most of the time, they don't mean what they say. And I said, "Besides, pal, the important people in your life—Jesus, your mom, your dad, your sister, and your friends—they all love you. They don't think you're weird. They think you are unique and wonderful and very important." Then we prayed again and hugged again and said goodnight. He was asleep before I went out the door.

PARENTING

A WIDE ANGLE VIEW

1 If the home where you grew up was a healing trauma center, describe a time you experienced healing from one of your parents.

Tell how you have tried to be a healing trauma center in your home and with your children.

A BIBLICAL PORTRAIT

Read Galatians 6:1–5

2 What lessons can be learned from this passage as we seek to make our homes a place of healing and wholeness?

3 What are some of the burdens kids carry today?

How do you determine which burdens to help them carry?

What can you do to make your home a place where your children feel free to bring their hurts, struggles, and burdens?

SHARPENING THE FOCUS

Read Snapshot "A Qualified Staff"

A QUALIFIED STAFF

The first component necessary for making your home a properly-functioning trauma center is a qualified staff. Medical trauma centers are only as effective as their staff. Home trauma centers are only as effective as the quality level of the parents. Here is a short excerpt from a letter I received some years ago. A woman writes: "In our family we were taught to be seen and not heard. I was told countless times by my parents how stupid I was. We were never allowed to show our emotions, so we stuffed them deep inside. We were taught the importance of putting on our 'Everything is fine face' before we went out in public. Fear, anger, and sorrow filled my young life." It is clear her parents did not have good training and education in healthy parenting skills. We all need to develop and sharpen our skills as parents on a regular basis.

4 There are some specific things you need to do to sharpen your healing abilities if you are going to make your home a healing trauma center where children can grow up whole and healthy. How are you seeking to do each of the four things listed below?

- Educating yourself in the skills of parenting through the many resources available today. What is one book, video, or other resource you have found helpful?

- Communicating to each child that they are treasured and valuable to you and to God.

- Helping your children learn to express their emotions rather than stuff them down inside.

- Challenging your kids not to put on false appearances but to be authentic.

Read Snapshot "Making Yourself Accessible"

MAKING YOURSELF ACCESSIBLE

If you're going to be a qualified staff person in the home trauma unit you need to be accessible. I learned this lesson in a powerful way when I spent a week down in South America teaching at a missionary school. One of the common denominators of the high school students I was teaching was that most of the kids' parents were out serving in a mission field far away. These students, as a rule, saw their parents for ten days over Christmas and six weeks in the summer. That was it. No other parental involvement.

It was the most difficult group of young people that I have ever spoken to in my life. It took me four days just to get their attention. By the fifth day I felt we finally established enough trust for some positive things to happen spiritually. Throughout the week I talked to discouraged and frustrated young people. Many were profoundly bitter. They didn't have a mom and dad to show them love, help heal their wounds, and wipe away the tears that every child sheds. In other words, they went to the trauma center when they were wounded, only to find a big "Closed" sign on the door.

5 Take a few minutes to honestly reflect on your own schedule and lifestyle. How much time do you spend in a normal week doing the following things:

Activity	*Hours spent*
Playing with your children	_____
Talking with your children about things that matter to them	_____
Praying, reading the Bible, and talking about spiritual things with your children	_____
Sitting down for a meal with your children	_____
Hanging around with your children with no agenda or schedule	_____

Tell your group what you learned about yourself and your personal accessibility through this reflection.

6

If you need to make yourself more available and accessible to your children, what needs to change in your schedule for this to happen?

How can your group members pray for you, support you, and keep you accountable as you grow in this area of your parenting?

Read Snapshot "The Importance of Being Observant"

THE IMPORTANCE OF BEING OBSERVANT

Quality staff members in the home trauma unit are observant. They are very careful in their diagnostic analysis to make sure they are getting to the root of the problem. They don't just gloss over the symptoms. As parents, we must be careful to observe the conduct and attitudes of our children. Early detection and treatment of some illnesses can reduce the likelihood of major disasters later. We need to watch for mood swings, expressions of frustration (no matter how small or subtle), changes in behavior patterns, or anything else that might indicate that our kids need some special care.

7

Why is it critical to learn how to be keenly observant of behaviors, words, and attitudes when it comes to your children?

What are some of the signs or signals your kids put out when they are hurting?

8

How do you respond to your kids in a time of crisis?

What prayer needs do they have at this time?

How can your group members support you as you care for your children?

PUTTING YOURSELF IN THE PICTURE

BECOMING BURDEN BEARERS

Identify a burden being carried by one of your children. What can you do over the coming month to help share the load of that burden? Come alongside of them and let them know you see the load they are carrying and that you want to help them with it. Sit down with one of your children and tell them about a burden *you* are carrying. Ask them to pray for you and let them know what they can do to help you with the load you are carrying. It's amazing how children open up and share their burdens when their parents lead the way.

BECOMING ACCESSIBLE

After evaluating your schedule, identify when you can spend more time with your children. Try to set a date with each child in the coming month for some one-on-one time. Do something that leaves a door open for discussion. Maybe you can take them out for an ice cream cone or a walk in the park. Find something you will both enjoy and just enjoy being together.

TEACHING FAITH IN THE HOME

REFLECTIONS FROM SESSION 5

1. If you have been seeking to help a child bear a burden, how have you seen their load grow lighter? What has this unified effort done for your relationship? If you asked one of your children to help you bear a burden, how did they respond?
2. What have you been doing to make yourself more accessible to your children? How have they been responding to your being more available to them?

THE BIG PICTURE

Have you ever taken time to scan the course of the first twenty years of your life and identify some of the significant spiritual memories you carry in your heart? Do you remember experiences, events, or conversations that made a lasting impression on your spiritual life? I call these important times "spiritual moments."

My most memorable "spiritual moments" did not happen in the course of the hundred of hours that I spent in Sunday School classes, youth groups, or Christian schools. Don't get me wrong. I treasure that part of my heritage and strongly recommend parents give careful consideration to involving their children in the various ministries that can be profitable for children. However, my most vivid spiritual moments, the ones that made the deepest marks on my life, were experiences that occurred within the context of my family.

One of my earliest "spiritual moments" came when I was in third or fourth grade. My uncle, my dad's brother, died suddenly of a massive heart attack. It was the first funeral I ever attended. I don't remember much about the memorial service at the church, but I can vividly remember standing at the graveside in a driving snowstorm in southwestern Michigan. I remember the pastor making his final remarks, closing with prayer, and the crowd of people starting to disperse.

I was shivering from the cold, and I looked through those driving snowflakes and I saw my dad reach into his pocket, take out a Bible, and walk over to the chair where his mother was sitting. This dear woman had already lost her husband and two other boys. My dad sat down in a chair next to her, put his arm on her shoulder, and read her Psalm 23: "The Lord is my Shepherd . . . I have everything I need."

What a memory! Even as a little guy, I thought to myself, "Something very important is going on right now." I learned that when all of life caves in, we turn to the Lord. We turn to the Good Shepherd who walks with us through the valley of the shadow of death. I remember thinking, "My father is a very strong man, and here he is turning to God's Word for comfort and encouragement when the roof of life has come crashing down." I remember deciding that I too would turn to the Lord when I faced times of need.

A WIDE ANGLE VIEW

1 Describe a spiritual moment you remember experiencing while growing up.

What lesson did you learn from this experience?

A BIBLICAL PORTRAIT

Read Deuteronomy 32:44–47

2 Why is it essential for the home to be the primary place where faith is learned?

Why is spiritual maturity in the lives of parents so important if the home is really the primary place where faith is learned?

SHARPENING THE FOCUS

Read Snapshot "A Dynamic Relationship with God"

A DYNAMIC RELATIONSHIP WITH GOD

We need to be careful that our kids don't start to think Christianity is merely a system of standards they have to live up to. It's too easy for children to reduce Christianity to just a set of rules and codes and standards. We need to do everything in our power to teach them that the essence of Christianity is a living and dynamic relationship with a loving God, where conversations flow back and forth as easily as a conversation with a close friend, where they can talk to God through prayer and expect Him to speak to them through His Holy Spirit. They need to know what it is to feel a sense of divine companionship all throughout the day because they are in a living relationship with God. They need to discover that Christianity is a living, dynamic, growing relationship with God and not just a set of rules and codes and standards.

---

3 How do we, as parents, sometimes give our children the impression that faith is about works and following religious rules and regulations?

4 What can we do to help our kids learn that being a
follower of Christ is about developing a living and
dynamic relationship with Jesus through:

- Our words

- Our lifestyle

- Our habits

- The way we approach worship

Read Snapshot "Serving God"

SERVING GOD

Children need to learn that service to God is one of the most satisfying experiences in all of life. We need to spare our children from squandering their lives by desperately searching for fulfillment in things that don't satisfy. Many adults today have to honestly admit that they have wasted many years trying to acquire that one elusive possession or trying to achieve that long-awaited goal or experience. Along the way we have discovered that none of these acquisitions, achievements, and experiences really satisfied. We need to help our children discover the joy and satisfaction that comes not from things, but from serving and following God.

5 What can parents do to show their children that
service is an essential and joyous part of being a
Christ follower?

How does serving God bring you satisfaction and joy?

6

What is an area of service you could enter into with
one of your kids?

*What could be gained through serving God in partnership
with your kids?*

Read Snapshot "Rich Rewards"

RICH REWARDS

We need to teach our kids that obeying God brings rich rewards. Our children should not grow up believing that Dad and Mom always know best. The fact is, we don't! They need to be convinced that God knows best. He really does. Our children need to know there are reasons for the restrictions we find in His Book, and that those reasons are valid. Our kids must understand that God is deeply concerned about their welfare and wants His best for them. They need to discover that there is unparalleled wisdom and guidance in His Word. We need to do all we can to help our children know that obeying God will result in a blessed life, but that disobeying Him will eventually shipwreck their lives.

7

Tell your group about a person in your life who has
modeled a deep love for God's Word.

*How did their commitment to reading and obeying God's
Word impact their life?*

8

What can you do to deepen your commitment to
study and obey God's Word?

*What can you do to help your children grow in their love for
God's Word?*

PUTTING YOURSELF IN THE PICTURE

BUILDING INTO YOUR RELATIONSHIP WITH GOD

If you are going to help your children grow in their faith, you
need to be in a dynamic and vibrant relationship with Jesus.
What can you do in the coming month to build your relationship with God? Do you need to set aside a time each day to
read the Bible, pray, and journal? Do you need to have a deeper commitment to attend worship with other followers of
Christ? What can you do to help your children grow in their
faith? Think specifically about the opportunities you have at
family meals. How can you use these times as an opportunity
to help your children grow in faith?

SERVING GOD

What is one specific act of service you can offer to God in
partnership with one of your children? Invite one of your children to enter into this ministry opportunity with you. Pray for
both of you to discover the joy and satisfaction that comes
from serving God.

LEADER'S NOTES

Leading a Bible discussion—especially for the first time—can make you feel both nervous and excited. If you are nervous, realize that you are in good company. Many biblical leaders, such as Moses, Joshua, and the apostle Paul, felt nervous and inadequate to lead others (see, for example, 1 Corinthians 2:3). Yet God's grace was sufficient for them, just as it will be for you.

Some excitement is also natural. Your leadership is a gift to the others in the group. Keep in mind, however, that other group members also share responsibility for the group. Your role is simply to stimulate discussion by asking questions and encouraging people to respond. The suggestions listed below can help you to be an effective leader.

PREPARING TO LEAD

1. Ask God to help you understand and apply the passage to your own life. Unless that happens, you will not be prepared to lead others.
2. Carefully work through each question in the study guide. Meditate and reflect on the passage as you formulate your answers.
3. Familiarize yourself with the leader's notes for each session. These will help you understand the purpose of the session and will provide valuable information about the questions in the session.
4. Pray for the various members of the group. Ask God to use these sessions to make you better disciples of Jesus Christ.
5. Before the first session, make sure each person has a study guide. Encourage them to prepare beforehand for each session.

LEADING THE SESSION

1. Begin the session on time. If people realize that the session begins on schedule, they will work harder to arrive on time.
2. At the beginning of your first time together, explain that these sessions are designed to be discussions, not lectures. Encourage everyone to participate, but realize some may be hesitant to speak during the first few sessions.

3. Don't be afraid of silence. People in the group may need time to think before responding.

4. Avoid answering your own questions. If necessary, rephrase a question until it is clearly understood. Even an eager group will quickly become passive and silent if they think the leader will do most of the talking.

5. Encourage more than one answer to each question. Ask, "What do the rest of you think?" or "Anyone else?" until several people have had a chance to respond.

6. Try to be affirming whenever possible. Let people know you appreciate their insights into the passage.

7. Never reject an answer. If it is clearly wrong, ask, "Which verse led you to that conclusion?" Or let the group handle the problem by asking them what they think about the question.

8. Avoid going off on tangents. If people wander off course, gently bring them back to the passage being considered.

9. Conclude your time together with conversational prayer. Ask God to help you apply those things that you learned in the session.

10. End on time. This will be easier if you control the pace of the discussion by not spending too much time on some questions or too little on others.

We encourage all small group leaders to use *Leading Life-Changing Small Groups* (Zondervan) by Bill Donahue while leading their group. Developed and used by Willow Creek Community Church, this guide is an excellent resource for training and equipping followers of Christ to effectively lead small groups. It includes valuable information on how to utilize fun and creative relationship-building exercises for your group; how to plan your meeting; how to share the leadership load by identifying, developing, and working with an "apprentice leader"; and how to find creative ways to do group prayer. In addition, the book includes material and tips on handling potential conflicts and difficult personalities, forming group covenants, inviting new members, improving listening skills, studying the Bible, and much more. Using *Leading Life-Changing Small Groups* will help you create a group that members love to be a part of.

Now let's discuss the different elements of this small group study guide and how to use them for the session portion of your group meeting.

THE BIG PICTURE

Each session will begin with a short story or overview of the lesson theme. This is called "The Big Picture" because it introduces the central theme of the session. You will need to read this section as a group or have group members read it on their own before discussion begins. Here are three ways you can approach this section of the small group session:

- As the group leader, read this section out loud for the whole group and then move into the questions in the next section, "A Wide Angle View." (You might read the first week, but then use the other two options below to encourage group involvement.)
- Ask a group member to volunteer to read this section for the group. This allows another group member to participate. It is best to ask someone in advance to give them time to read over the section before reading it to the group. It is also good to ask someone to volunteer, and not to assign this task. Some people do not feel comfortable reading in front of a group. After a group member has read this section out loud, move into the discussion questions.
- Allow time at the beginning of the group for each person to read this section silently. If you do this, be sure to allow enough time for everyone to finish reading so they can think about what they've read and be ready for meaningful discussion.

A WIDE ANGLE VIEW

This section includes one or more questions that move the group into a general discussion of the session topic. These questions are designed to help group members begin discussing the topic in an open and honest manner. Once the topic of the lesson has been established, move on to the Bible passage for the session.

A BIBLICAL PORTRAIT

This portion of the session includes a Scripture reading and one or more questions that help group members see how the theme of the session is rooted and based in biblical teaching. The Scripture reading can be handled just like "The Big Picture" section: You can read it for the group, have a group member read it, or allow time for silent reading. Make sure everyone has a Bible or that you have Bibles available for those who need them. Once you have read the passage, ask the question(s) in this section so that group members can dig into the truth of the Bible.

SHARPENING THE FOCUS

The majority of the discussion questions for the session are in this section. These questions are practical and help group members apply biblical teaching to their daily lives.

SNAPSHOTS

The "Snapshots" in each session help prepare group members for discussion. These anecdotes give additional insight to the topic being discussed. Each "Snapshot" should be read at a designated point in the session. This is clearly marked in the session as well as in the leader's notes. Again, follow the same format as you do with "The Big Picture" section and the "Biblical Portrait" section: Either you read the anecdote, have a group member volunteer to read, or provide time for silent reading. However you approach this section, you will find these anecdotes very helpful in triggering lively dialogue and moving discussion in a meaningful direction.

PUTTING YOURSELF IN THE PICTURE

Here's where you roll up your sleeves and put the truth into action. This portion is very practical and action-oriented. At the end of each session there will be suggestions for one or two ways group members can put what they've just learned into practice. Review the action goals at the end of each session and challenge group members to work on one or more of them in the coming week.

You will find follow-up questions for the "Putting Yourself in the Picture" section at the beginning of the next week's session. Starting with the second week, there will be time set aside at the beginning of the session to look back and talk about how you have tried to apply God's Word in your life since your last time together.

PRAYER

You will want to open and close your small group with a time of prayer. Occasionally, there will be specific direction within a session for how you can do this. Most of the time, however, you will need to decide the best place to stop and pray. You may want to pray or have a group member volunteer to begin the session with a prayer. Or you might want to read "The Big Picture" and discuss the "Wide Angle View" questions before opening in prayer. In some cases, it might be best to open in prayer after you have read the Bible passage. You need to decide where you feel an opening prayer best fits for your group.

When opening in prayer, think in terms of the session theme and pray for group members (including yourself) to be responsive to the truth of Scripture and the working of the Holy Spirit. If you have seekers in your group (people investigating Christianity but not yet believers) be sensitive to your expectations for group prayer. Seekers may not yet be ready to take part in group prayer.

Be sure to close your group with a time of prayer as well. One option is for you to pray for the entire group. Or you might allow time for group members to offer audible prayers that others can agree with in their hearts. Another approach would be to allow a time of silence for one-on-one prayers with God and then to close this time with a simple "Amen."

TO BE OR NOT TO BE

COLOSSIANS 3:18—21

INTRODUCTION

Why is the topic of parenting so important? Because all people—young and old—matter to God. God is deeply concerned about how children are raised and treated by their parents. Some people are whole and healthy and seem to be able to move into parenting with relative ease. However, there are many people who carry deep scars, and their personal woundedness makes parenting a potentially dangerous proposition.

This session encourages us to be very wise and prayerful before we decide to have children. It also give a caution to those who encourage others to jump into parenthood without honestly evaluating the health of their marriage and their personal wholeness. If we are going to raise whole children, we need to have a solid marriage relationship and a certain degree of personal health and wholeness.

This is not the time in history to watch Brady Bunch reruns and romanticize about the endless bliss of children and family. It's a new day. We've got to face life realistically. Raising children today is going to require well-honed skills. Parents face greater demands on their time and resources, and are confronted with some of the most challenging parenting decisions that have ever faced any set of parents.

THE BIG PICTURE

Take time to read this introduction with the group. There are suggestions for how this can be done in the beginning of the leader's section.

A WIDE ANGLE VIEW

Question One These statements might bring some very divergent responses. Allow for honest communication and reflection on each statement. The key is to begin identifying that raising children is not as easy as it used to be. Our world has changed, and we need to realize that the climate for naturally raising healthy children is no longer with us. If we are going to raise whole children it will take real work, prayer, and energy.

A friend of mine who made a fortune in the media-related industry is fond of saying to others, "Anyone could have made a million dollars in my industry if he had hung his shingle in the late '60s and showed up most days for work." Now, obviously, he's being more than a little modest about his accomplishments. However, behind that statement he was really saying, "Look, the business environment, the economic factors, the cultural environment, and almost everything else was conducive for success in my particular industry at that time. All factors were favorable. So, if ten people started businesses in the late '60s in that part of the media industry, all ten would probably have flourished. But times have changed. The growth cycle is over, the climate is completely different. Conditions are no longer favorable for that industry. If ten people were to launch new businesses in that field today, it's very likely that only a couple of them could make it. And those who did would break their backs doing so."

Parenting in our day has many similar parallels. The climate has changed. The culture has changed. Easy child rearing no longer exists. It is tough going. Even committed marriage partners who are fairly healthy will have to work hard if they are going to raise whole and healthy children.

A BIBLICAL PORTRAIT

Read Colossians 3:18–21

Question Two The goal here is not to create a debate over the roles within the home. The focus should be on what a family would look like if there was mutual submission, love, and respect between all family members. This is God's plan and design for our families. Allow time for honest reflection on what a family might look like if we followed God's direction in this passage.

Question Three We live in a self-centered culture and time. We are taught to seek our own desires and to fulfill our dreams. When we enter into a marriage relationship, we discover self-centered living leads only to conflict and tension. If we are going to raise whole and healthy children, we must commit to having a healthy marriage relationship. Mutual love, respect, and submission in the home are essential for this to happen. Allow time for group members to reflect on those things that help and hinder the process of selfless love and living.

SHARPENING THE FOCUS

Read Snapshot "Times Have Changed" before Question 4

Question Five If you were to line up twenty-five marriage and family experts today and ask them if today's cultural climate is more or less conducive for raising children effectively, all twenty-five would cry in unison, "These are difficult days." Actually, the word perilous would be an accurate adjective.

Some time ago, in the *Chicago Tribune*, a guidance counselor at a local high school was interviewed. He had been serving in his position since 1966. The article begins, "It's a whole new ball game today. Twenty years ago," he said, "a few kids smoked a little bit of pot and would drink beer on Friday nights. But what goes on on Friday nights today is unbelievable. These days, guys and girls go out on Friday nights, have a few beers until 11:30, and then they have sex. Once in awhile they finish off the evening by trashing the house where they held the party. They did so recently in a house nearby and caused $10,000 worth of damage." The counselor went on to mention a few of the ways the world of high school students has changed in the last few decades. He mentioned that twenty years ago divorce wasn't that much of an issue. Its effects were basically still unfelt in the high schools. Drugs were new, and for the most part, untried. Alcohol was not widely abused. Sexually transmitted diseases were rarely even talked about, and no one had ever heard of AIDS.

Our world is changing. Rap groups scream obscenities in crowded concert halls, pornography is shown in movie theaters and condoms are distributed in high schools. It's a whole new world. It's a perilous time to be raising children—not at all! My point in all of this is not to discourage parents from having children. It is simply to bring a proper sense of sober-mindedness to bear on the decision. The childrearing challenge is becoming increasingly difficult and parents must take that into consideration as they discuss whether or not to have children, and if so, when. This should also lead to serious consideration of the number of children they are capable of raising effectively in today's world.

Read Snapshot "Wounded Parents" before Question 6

Question Six This could be a very vulnerable question for a group setting. If you feel your group can discuss this in a healthy way, use this in the context of the whole group. You may decide to have the men and women separate at this time and discuss question six in same-sex groups. Another option would be to have your group members reflect on this sixth question in couples. Use your own discernment for how to proceed with this question.

Be ready with resources if there are deep wounds communicated. There may be a need to help one or more of your group members move toward some Christian counseling to deal with some deep areas of pain and woundedness. Be ready to refer them to your own church counselor or a Christian counselor you know and trust. If you don't have resources to meet this area of need, talk with your pastor or someone on your church staff who can help you.

Read Snapshot "Three Critical Questions" before Question 7

Allow ten minutes for your group members to break up as couples and discuss the questions in the next section of this session. If you have some single parents, allow them to gather with other single parents or to take time for reflection on their own.

Question Seven Jesus said in Matthew 10:16, "Be as shrewd as snakes and as innocent as doves." In light of the present-day realities, it seems to me that wisdom and good judgment demand that would-be parents hold off on starting a family until three basic questions discussed in the above Snapshot are answered honestly.

The first of those questions focuses on whether the relationship between the husband and wife is solid enough to withstand the pressure that children add. In other words, is the foundation for the family strong enough to bear the load of having and raising children?

It's widely held that one of the single most important ingredients in the child-rearing challenge is for the husband and the wife to demonstrate a healthy, consistent, loving relationship toward each other. This is why the Bible puts so much emphasis on the need for husbands and wives to develop a true spirit of intimacy. There needs to be a spirit of trust and tenderness toward each other. A spirit of understanding and respect.

God designed the family to work so that the marriage relationship would be the foundation upon which the whole family would be built. From watching how their mom and dad relate, children eventually learn how love works. Where else are they going to learn these lessons? It is only in the home where children learn how trust works, how relational delight should be expressed to other people, how feelings ought to be communicated and received, how differences ought to be negotiated, how values ought to be formed and then courageously lived out, how conflict should be resolved, how Christianity should be lived inside and outside the church walls, how servanthood and mutual submission can lubricate a relationship. These and a host of other critical dynamics are gradually absorbed by the children by just hanging around the father and the mother and watching the marriage work.

As all of us know, a positive marital environment can contribute to a strong sense of personal security and a general emotional, spiritual, and psychological wholeness in the lives of children. However, a negative marital environment can cause terror, anxiety, insecurity, relational confusion, spiritual confusion, emotional chaos, and woundedness of unimaginable depth for the children who grow up in that kind of environment.

The application of this point is obvious: Would-be parents, for their own sake and especially for the sake of the children they're so anxious to have, would be wise to strengthen and develop their own marriage relationship to a point of relative maturity well before any thought of bringing children onto the scene.

Don't be deceived; the notion that having children will draw two struggling, estranged spouses *together* is simply *not the case*. It is more likely that children will put more pressure and strain on a marriage. Couples would do well to wait long enough to make sure that their marriage relationship is strong and healthy enough to provide a positive foundation for children to build their lives on.

Read Snapshot "Passing a Broken Baton" before Question 8

Question Eight Both husband and wife need to deal with their brokenness and wounds from their past before they unintentionally inflict those wounds on their children. I have often used, building on the theme of the relay race, the concept of passing a "broken baton." This is simply the understanding that if you grew up experiencing deep pain and brokenness, you will probably pass on to your children the legacy you received. If you were handed a broken baton, you will most likely pass on the same to your children—*unless* you have the courage to seek healing and wholeness first. As you experience healing from your woundedness, you can be transformed by God's healing power and become ready to pass on a legacy of blessedness to your children.

You might need to make a covenant with God and your spouse to stop the tragic cycle of generational injustice. You might need to commit yourself to face the pain of your past. This means you must be ready to feel your pain, understand it thoroughly, grieve authentically, process it fully, and open up to some trusted friends and, most of all, to God. You may need to get some Christian counseling to help you work through it. You might decide to hold off on starting a family until there's ample reason to believe that you'll be able to pass on a baton of blessedness to your children instead of a broken baton.

I have preached on this topic on numerous occasions. One time a young couple came up to me after the service. The husband was holding a little baby. He said, "Look at our treasure. Two years ago, we heard your message about not passing on a broken baton. We were all fired up to have kids. Boy, we wanted to have kids. But we went out to the parking lot after your message, looked at each other, and said, 'We're not ready.' We both went into Christian counseling and processed what it meant for both of us to have grown up in alcoholic homes. We've been working on our own issues and on our marriage since then. And we've come to a point of healing. Now we have this precious child and we want to pass on a baton of blessedness." I hope this story illustrates your desire as well.

Scripture is clear on whose responsibility it is to raise children. It's the responsibility of both parents. The full involvement of the father—emotionally and spiritually—is absolutely critical to the childrearing challenge. Detached or absent fathers wound children in ways that cause deep and lasting scars. Fathers have to be signed on for real engagement. It goes without saying that both moms and dads have to be prepared to make the substantial investments and sacrifices associated with having and raising children.

Some parents think they can "microwave" a child to maturity. Others hire somebody to raise their children for them while they continue to set sales records. Those options do not fulfill the biblical command for parents. Fathers and mothers need to make the raising of their children one of the highest priorities in their lives. You must be prepared to make whatever changes are necessary, including career adjustments, financial adjustments, and schedule adjustments in order to carry out the high call of being a parent.

If you make those kinds of sacrifices and if you follow the biblical plan for raising children, God has a way of returning a multiplied reward to parents. We discover there is fulfillment, community, security, and refuge in family life. What compares to the rewards of parenting?

For Lynne and me, God's leading for us to have children was clear. We don't have a single regret. However, all of us need to seek God honestly about these matters. You have to look at the world realistically, soberly. You have to ask tough questions about the strength of your marriage, about whether or not you've dealt fully with your own woundedness so that you're not going to pass a baton of brokenness on to your children but rather a baton of blessing. If you already have children and you realize you are passing on a baton of brokenness to them, it's not too late. Get help right now. If you process your woundedness, there's still time to turn it around, even if your kids are getting older. You can still begin a reparenting process.

Some couples, under the leading of the Holy Spirit, might decide to invest their lives in helping other families raise their children and not have children of their own. That's a private matter between them and the Lord. Who are we to put pressure on them one way or the other? Some couples may feel called to ministries or vocations that preclude the advisability of having children. That's a private matter between God and them. Proverbs 3:5–6 says, "Trust in the LORD with all your heart and lean not on your own understanding; in all your ways acknowledge him, and he will make your paths straight." When He directs it, follow it. You'll be glad you did.

PUTTING YOURSELF IN THE PICTURE

Let the group members know you will be providing time at the beginning of the next meeting for them to discuss how they have put their faith into action. Let them tell about how they have acted on one of the two options above. However, don't limit their interaction to these two options. They may have put themselves into the picture in some other way as a result of your study. Allow for honest and open communication.

Also, be clear that there will not be any kind of a "test" or forced reporting. All you are going to do is allow time for people to volunteer to talk about how they have applied what they learned in your last study. Some group members will feel pressured if they think you are going to make everyone report on how they acted on these action goals. You don't want anyone to skip the next meeting because they are afraid of having to say they did not follow up on what they learned from the prior session. The key is to provide a place for honest communication without creating pressure and fear of being embarrassed.

Every session from this point on will open with a look back at the "Putting Yourself in the Picture" section of the previous session.

RAISING WHOLE CHILDREN

DEUTERONOMY 6:4—9

INTRODUCTION

If I could choose four things for parents to impart to their children, here is what I would choose. First, I would want to see the parental ability to build a *strong sense of self-esteem*. Second, I would hope for parents to be able to develop a *sense of personal competence*. Third, I would want to see parents have the ability to develop *healthy relational skills* in their children. And fourth, and most important, I would long for the parental ability to *lay a spiritual foundation* for the next generation.

Some people might want to impart a parental ability to produce a millionaire by age thirty. Others would desire to have the parental ability to produce an Ivy League grad, a child star, or a super athlete. I'd stick with just the four abilities mentioned above because I firmly believe they represent the four broad areas that most enable a child to grow up whole and be prepared for this life and eternity. These four growth areas will be the focus of this small group interaction.

THE BIG PICTURE

Take time to read this introduction with the group. There are suggestions for how this can be done in the beginning of the leader's section.

A BIBLICAL PORTRAIT

Read Deuteronomy 6:4–9

Question Two If we are going to raise whole and healthy children, we need to be whole and healthy adults. The starting point of this wholeness is found in the words of Deuteronomy 6:5. We need to passionately love the Lord our God with all that is in us. If we are not actively taking steps to grow deeper in love with our God, we will not be ready to raise whole and healthy children.

SHARPENING THE FOCUS

Read Snapshot "Building Self-Esteem" before Question 4

Question Four If I ever begin to become a little numb or insensitive to how important it is for children to have a strong sense of their value, all I have to do is pull out a note from a folder I keep on file in my office. It's a true story about an eight-year-old boy named Robbie. He grew up in a home where the parents were not committed to building a sense of value into their children. He grew up in a home where the parents told him constantly that he was "good for nothin'." Somewhere along the way his parents had some trouble in their relationship. Their marriage began to fall apart, and Robbie concluded that he was probably the cause. So at eight years old, Robbie wrote his parents this letter.

> Dear Mom and Dad,
> I'm sorry I make you unhappy. I'm sorry I'm so bad. I'm sorry I'm no good. Maybe if I wasn't alive, Daddy, you would love Mommy. I'm so sorry. It's all my fault so I'm going to die. I love you.
> Robbie
> P.S. Teddy is with me because he loves me even when I'm bad.

After writing that note in crayon to his parents, Robbie swallowed a whole bottle of aspirin, clutched his teddy bear to his chest, and lay down to die. Fortunately, Robbie was rescued and received medical attention, but he had to be committed to a psychiatric ward for a long, long time.

What was wrong with this young boy? He felt like he was an interruption. He felt like he was a problem. He saw himself as a liability and not an asset. He had a total lack of self-esteem—a sense of worthlessness that cut so deep that death became a better option than life.

Parents must never underestimate how desperately children crave to be loved, valued, and told they're important and treasured. Don't trivialize or discount the importance of building self-esteem into your children, regardless of how old they are.

When you seek to build self-esteem in your children, remember these three things: a word, a look, and a touch.

A Word. Parenting is powerful. It creates or destroys children through words. A friend of mine wrote these words to me recently: "My parents destroyed me with their words. It's taken years of sweat and toil and thousands of dollars worth of counseling to recuperate." He said, "If God ever entrusts children to me, you can bet they are going to hear affirmations all the time." Parents need to understand the power of their words to build up or tear down children. Then they need to commit to building up. Say "I love you!" a hundred times and then say it five hundred times. Say it a thousand times and then say it ten thousand times. "Jason, I love you!" "Jennifer, you're precious to me." "Mike, you are a great kid." "Heather, you bring more joy to me than I ever thought a human heart could contain. Oh, how you bring joy to me." "Matt, if I could custom design a little guy, pick out everything I wanted in a son, I would pick out a boy about your height and weight with hair like yours and a face like yours and strong little arms like yours and legs that run just like your legs run. I'd pick a kid who laughs and cries like you do. Matt, I'd choose you out of a line of a million little guys. You need to know your dad is nuts about you."

Remember, God the Father at Jesus' baptism? Jesus is standing in front of a multitude about ready to launch His earthly ministry. Everything is quiet and the words come from God the Father in heaven: "This is my Son, whom I love; with him I am well pleased" (Matt. 3:17).

A Look. Looks of love can become permanent photographs in the mental scrapbook that your kids carry around in their heads for the rest of their lives. Just look at them now and then and let them see the delight in your eyes—the warmth, the affection. Looks are powerful. At the same time, be very careful not to gun them down with angry stares or cut into them with eyes like daggers. We communicate a great deal with our eyes and the looks we give people. Our children take these pictures into their minds and hearts. We need to look at them with tenderness and love.

A Touch. Fathers need to hear this more than most mothers, but all parents need an occasional reminder about the importance of a loving touch. Don't let a day go by without giving your children—of any age—an appropriate, affectionate touch. If your kids are young, chase them around, gather them up, hold them, and smother them with affection. We use to call those "love attacks" around our house. My kids would see that look in my eye as I was coming after them for one of those love attacks, and they'd take off running. But they would always make sure they got caught. Obviously, appropriate touch changes over the years. But parents can always affirm the value of a child by tender touches that send signals of affirmation and affection that are not soon forgotten.

One Sunday morning after a church service I saw a man with a son in his late twenties walking out into the lobby. As they walked side by side I saw the man put his arm around the shoulder of his son. The son slipped his arm around the back of the dad. That's powerful!

Read Snapshot "Developing a Sense of Personal Competence" before Question 5

Question Five Do a study sometime of the backgrounds of some highly competent people. Usually you will find that these people had parents who trained and challenged their children to develop and stretch their talents early on in life. I'm not advocating prenatal consciousness training or flash cards in the maternity ward. But it's an established fact that if parents take the time to train, instruct, coach, and inspire their children early on, these children learn to be more competent. They are able to fail and succeed with more confidence. I think developing a strong sense of competence and ability in the lives of young children is one of the most crucial tests of effective parenting.

I hope and pray my children will develop the self-confidence to be able to say convincingly to themselves, "I have some skills and smarts. I can think through a problem. I can come up with ways to get things done even if there are roadblocks. I can hang in there until the job gets done. It might take me awhile, but I probably will be able to do it. I can compete and hold my own."

Read Snapshot "Developing Relational Skills" before Question 6

Question Six It is critically important for parents to help their children develop strong relational skills. A central part of this is helping them learn to communicate well, which includes talking about feelings. Take time as a group and develop some good discussion questions that are age appropriate for children of various ages. After you have come up with some good questions, try them out on each other. Then, encourage group members to also try them out on young people in their life.

The lack of relational and communicational skills is one of the reasons so many young people are becoming sexually active at unthinkable ages. When they're with members of the opposite sex, they simply don't know what else to do. They've never learned the conversational skills that are necessary to begin a valid friendship. They don't know how to have meaningful dialogue. They don't know how to ask or answer the kinds of questions that would enable them to build a foundation for a relationship.

Question Seven Parents, now more than ever, need to teach and model relational skills. Kids aren't prepared for life without them. And they'll never be whole unless they have them.

Here are some practical suggestions on how to do this.

Get in the habit of asking your children questions that force them to discuss their feelings. Instead of just asking "How did you do on your math test, Mike?" Ask a follow-up question. "How did you feel about getting a C–? How did you feel about getting a B+, Mike? Were you glad about it? Pretty fired up about it? Were you embarrassed? Were you angry about it? Frustrated? Tell me how you feel about it." Instead of saying, "How did it go at school today, Jen?" Instead of settling for a one-word answer, why not say "Jen, what's going on in your friendships at school? Do your friends make you feel good? How are you feeling about school? Do you like it? Do you hate it? Are you frustrated with it?" Convince them that you really want to know about their feelings. You might have to draw this information out of them at first. You might have to help them with some word choices and some descriptions of feelings, but those kinds of conversations go a long way toward building your children's relational skills. They learn the art of dialogue, of expression, of communication. And might I add, be sure to express some of how *you* feel when they ask you about your day, your work, your life.

Model what to do when a relationship gets bruised or broken. Over the years, Lynne and I have decided to acknowledge the fact that marriage requires a certain number of hard talks and struggles in order to keep it in line. We don't hide this reality from our children. I don't want them growing up thinking it's all marital bliss. I don't want to always go in the bedroom and close the door or go out to dinner to have conflict resolution talks apart from them. I want them to get in the habit of seeing that Mom and Dad have to work through issues once in awhile to make a marriage work. I want them to know that all relationships are subject to rough waters and are subject to bruises and breakdowns. They need to see and learn from healthy conflict resolution.

**Read Snapshot "The Spiritual Dimension of Life"
before Question 8**

PUTTING YOURSELF IN THE PICTURE

Challenge group members to take time in the coming week to
use part or all of this application section as an opportunity for
continued growth.

AFFIRMING EACH CHILD'S UNIQUENESS

PSALM 139:1—18

INTRODUCTION

This session is about discerning and discovering the uniqueness of your children. Every child is wired a little differently and parents need to discover and affirm what is unique in each child. The differences reside primarily in the areas of temperament, motivated interests and abilities, and the way they express and receive love. The theory that kids are just lumps of clay to be molded by their parents has lost its shine in recent years. We realize that all kids are not alike. They have their own characteristics and bents that are begging to be expressed. In this study we will discover how to recognize the uniqueness of each child and how to encourage each one to develop his or her distinct personality and approach to life. It's time for parents to stop trying to mold and shape children into some preset notion of what parents think children should be. God makes each person distinct. We need to discover these unique qualities and nurture them.

THE BIG PICTURE

Take time to read this introduction with the group. There are suggestions for how this can be done in the beginning of the leader's section.

A WIDE ANGLE VIEW

Question One Several years ago Shauna and Todd and I were coming home from church on a Sunday. As I listened to their conversation, I grew increasingly concerned about the content and the tone of it. I didn't like what I was hearing communicated between my two kids. The more I listened to it, the angrier I got. By the time we drove up our driveway, I was letting them have it with both barrels.

Shauna was sitting in the front seat and Todd was in the back. I could tell that even my double-barrel diatribe was not fazing Shauna all that much. So, I took it up another notch. I did the old "I am sick and tired . . ." and "If I ever, ever, ever . . ." and "so help me." I let them both have it! By the time I finished, Shauna was humble. She wasn't broken. She wasn't bent over with remorse or promising never to do it again. But she was humble enough for my satisfaction. As she slipped into the house, I said to myself, "Well, that took some doing, but she got the point. Nice job, Dad. A lot of guys would not have had the courage to do what I did. It's tough to raise a strong-willed child, but I hung in there. She's lucky to have a dad like me."

Right about then I saw Todd staggering around the back of the car. I almost forgot he was in the car. When I saw him, I knew in an instant that what I said had devastated him. His face was contorted and there was a look of sadness and shame that was not good. He was sobbing, "Dad, I'm sorry, I'm sorry, I'm sorry." In that heart-piercing moment of time, I knew parental pain on a deeper level than I had ever known it before. I had gone too far for him. Then, as if my regret weren't profound enough, he came right toward me and wrapped his arms around me and kept sobbing, "Dad, I'm so sorry, I'm so sorry, I'm so sorry." And not only was Todd hurting—I was a wreck for the rest of the day.

It was a sterling example of the dangers of treating very different kids the very same way. I remember going back to my study and telling Lynne all about it. I said, "Lynne, if I discipline these kids exactly the same way, both kids are in for real heartbreak because they're so different." Shauna is very strong. She needs strong confrontation and discipline because of the way she's wired. Todd only requires a mild reprimand. And if that isn't followed immediately by expressions of love and affirmation, his spirit can be crushed. From that memorable day forward, Lynne and I have done everything in our power to discern the uniqueness in our children and to modify our parental approach as we take those differences into consideration.

A Biblical Portrait

Read Psalm 139:1–18

Question Three If we are going to affirm the uniqueness of our children, we need to begin by seeing them as God sees them. They matter to God and He loves them deeply. He has molded and shaped them. He has wired them in a way that is unique.

It might be hard for some parents to appreciate the uniqueness of their children because they have a hard time seeing themselves as valuable to God. Parents need to see themselves as "fearfully and wonderfully made." This passage and the discussion that can follow will help group members articulate how each of us is unique and wonderful.

Read Snapshot "Affirming Each Child's Unique Temperament" before Question 4

Questions Four and Five There can be so many temperamental differences in children born into the same family. One child can be a social butterfly . . . never happy unless there are lots of people around to relate to. Another child in the same family can prefer to play alone for hours on end. One child lines up his toys in neat rows and keeps his things in order. The other child in the same family is dedicated to total disarray. This child seems to be committed to being chaotic and disorganized.

I remember sitting in a restaurant years ago when my children were young. Todd took all the little jelly containers out of the jelly racks, put them on the table, organized them by flavor, and put them back in the little holder. He couldn't figure out why the management would tolerate jumbled up jellies. Across the table Shauna was mixing tea with coffee and cream and sugar and experimenting with a new creative blend.

One child in a family is laid-back and easy-going. Another is high-strung, worrisome, and needs to know all the details. "When are we going? Where are we going? When are we going to be back? Tell me, Mom. Tell me, Dad." These are just examples of God-given temperament differences. One child loves taking risks. New challenges are greeted with "Let me go first, Dad. Let me try." Another child is faced with a new challenge and says, "Not me, Mom. Not in a million years." That child is fearful and approaches every new challenge with great apprehension. One child comes through the door at the end of the day and spills every single thought and feeling on the table. Another child is quiet and so hesitant to discuss his or her feelings that you end up having to pull out information and feelings. How do you explain all these differences, except to say that in God's good pleasure, He wires each of us differently and gives different temperaments and personalities as He sees fit.

Effective parenting demands that we not only study our children enough to discern their uniqueness, but that we affirm them as well. We need to express delight in their differences and celebrate them. In so doing, we give each of our children the assurance that God wired them up the way He did because He wanted someone on the earth to reflect His image through their exact personality and temperament arrangement.

But be honest, parents. It's easier said than done. How easy is it for an energetic, extroverted, dynamic mother to really affirm and celebrate a shy, reserved, introverted daughter? Isn't it tempting for a "wonder woman" to want to have a "wonder daughter"? How easy is it for a high-risk, fiercely competitive father to really find delight in an easy-going, laid-back son who just doesn't have the killer instinct? It's not very easy for parents who are wired up one way to really delight in a child who is wired differently. But parents, if you understand the creative genius of God and if you appreciate the fact that God doesn't mass produce anything, you will learn how to affirm the uniqueness in the lives of your children. Celebrate each one of them.

When parents communicate a sense of delight in the way God wired up each of their children, that delight unleashes a positive and powerful dynamic that serves them well throughout life and eternity. Isn't it worth some thought and prayer? Isn't it worth a breakfast or a dinner where the parents go out and work up a kind of temperament profile on each of the children, discuss the differences, and then work diligently with God's help to affirm those differences and to celebrate them?

Read Snapshot "Affirming Interests and Abilities" before Question 6

Question Six Parents, it's decision time. We're at a crossroads. When we discover what really fires up our kids, what their motivated passions and interests are, we can either affirm their passions and coach them in that direction, or we can attempt to extinguish them. We can either celebrate their enthusiasm over these motivated abilities and interests and seek to further their fired-up feelings, or we can impose our interests and our agendas on them.

Having seen the results of both approaches, I'll choose the affirmation route any day. The fact that I am a pastor of a church goes back to a time over two decades ago when I stood in my father's office and said, "Dad, I know that you've worked all your adult life to build a company that you could hand to me and my brother. But I have to tell you, it's not where my passions lie. It's not what fires me up. I feel God is calling me to do something else." How grateful I am for a father who looked at me with sadness on one side of his heart and support on the other. He said, "Bill, you've got to go and follow what you're excited about." One of the first things I want to do when I get to heaven is thank my father for affirming what I was interested in. He freed me to leave something he was fired up about so I could do what God called me to do and what He gave me a love for doing.

You know, I was thinking the other day, it would devastate me to hear either of my kids say to me someday "Dad, I lived the life you laid out for me, but I never lived the life God laid out for me." The thought of that makes me tremble. I'm hoping that someday my kids will say, "Dad, thanks for exposing us to a wide range of life experiences. Thanks for observing and discussing our reactions, coaching us a little bit. Thanks for affirming us in the direction of our own God-given passions— not yours or Mom's. Thanks for celebrating our unique callings and our concerns and for sparing us from yours. Thanks for trusting God in the whole process. Thanks for not taking matters into your own hands, but leaving them in God's hands." I would love to hear those words someday. I think that's the stuff all of us parents want to hear. But in order for us hear those words, we have to discover the unique callings, interests, and passions of our kids and then coach them in the direction that God is leading.

Read Snapshot "The Language of Love" before Question 7

Question Eight The challenge is twofold. First, determine which language each of our children prefers to receive, a language that they want you to speak in order for them to feel loved. This is no small task. It often requires a lot of observation, experimentation, and communication. It probably varies with each child. But each child has a preferred way of receiving love from you.

For some it is a hug or physical affection. For others it is a word or a note reminding them how much they are loved. For others it may be a special little gift, or maybe time alone with you. It varies from person to person.

The second part of the challenge is to learn to speak the particular language they tune into best. This can require our becoming multilingual. The temptation is to say, "I'll show my love by providing material things for them or by doing laundry and making their lunches." We need to be careful not to force them to speak our language. Instead, we need to learn to become fluent in their language.

What about that daughter who yearns to be embraced and can't believe she is truly loved unless someone has their arms around her on a regular basis? What about her? Some of you have daughters like that. They've been love starved their whole lives. You can speak lovingly to them, you can give them gifts, you can provide exciting opportunities. If their love language is that they need to be held, and if you're not holding them, it breaks their hearts. What really worries me about daughters who love to be held is that if they don't get the right kind of holding from Mom and Dad, when they get to be sophomores in high school, they'll be held by any guy who comes around with outstretched arms. Sadly, many times he's the wrong guy.

What about the son who will never feel loved unless somebody spends large chunks of time with him? What about him? You can give him gifts, tell him you love him, hug him until he's blue. But if he's wired up to need to receive large blocks of time to authenticate your love, then hanging out with him is what is going to say "I love you."

If we address and achieve this twofold challenge of learning each child's preferred style of love language and becoming fluent in it, then we're really going to connect with each of our children in ways that will bond us with them for a lifetime.

Take this seriously. Study each of your children, experiment with a variety of expressions of love, and see which language your children respond to best and then, for their sake, try speaking their language. When you begin to see the responsiveness in each of your children, you'll thank God a thousand times for awakening you to the need to discern and speak each child's love language.

Parents, we only have our children for a season. Let's covenant together to give them memories, to give them treasures that they can carry with them throughout life and eternity.

PUTTING YOURSELF IN THE PICTURE

Challenge group members to take time in the coming week to use part or all of this application section as an opportunity for continued growth.

MISTAKES PARENTS MAKE

PROVERBS 13:24; 22:15

INTRODUCTION

We all make mistakes. We can laugh at most of them when some time passes. But some mistakes are different. Some mistakes don't get funnier as time passes. Some mistakes get increasingly tragic. Many parental mistakes fall into this category. You know how it goes. Little Tommy's temper was cute at age two. Too cute for the parents to worry about. Too cute to correct. It wasn't nearly as cute at age twelve when Tommy kept getting detentions at school for fighting. When he gave his wife a black eye at age twenty-two, that wasn't cute at all. When he threw his son through a screen door at age thirty-two, then humor had turned to horror. Many parental mistakes are like that. They don't get funnier over time. The years tend to multiply the consequences of our parenting mistakes.

In this study I want to zero in on three mistakes parents seem to make with alarming frequency. These mistakes usually have to do with the *discipline* process, how *feelings* are handled in the home, and how *character* and inner strength are developed in the lives of children. If we can learn early in the process of raising children, we can spare them from many heartaches in the future.

THE BIG PICTURE

Take time to read this introduction with the group. There are suggestions for how this can be done in the beginning of the leader's section.

A WIDE ANGLE VIEW

Question One We all have embarrassing moments in our lives. Take time as a group to tell some of your stories. They don't have to be about parenting. If you need more help getting the ball rolling, you may want to tell the story below.

I was with a group of athletes one time, and things got a little slow so I asked them if they would tell me about an embarrassing situation in their past. One guy told a story about an experience he had in high school as a third-string basketball player. He spent most of his time on the bench down by the cheerleaders. But at his senior homecoming game, quite a few players got fouled out. He thought to himself, "I might get in this game. My family and friends are here. My homecoming date might finally get a chance to see me play." His heart is pumping and his hands are getting all sweaty. The fourth quarter comes and the game is close. Sure enough, the second-string guard fouls out. The coach looks right in his eyes and says, "You, get in the game." He's so fired up that he tears off his warm-up jacket and his warm-up pants and dashes out on the floor. Then he feels a strange breeze. He had pulled off more than his warm-up pants and there he was standing at center court in his athletic supporter. *That's* an embarrassing moment!

A BIBLICAL PORTRAIT

Read Proverbs 13:24 and 22:15

Questions Two & Three The Bible says that all children desperately need discipline. Just read Proverbs 22:15. The Bible teaches that because of the very real presence of sin and evil in the nature of human beings, children are born with a bent toward rebellion, self-centeredness, and self-promotion. Children are born with a readiness to lie, cheat, and manipulate. They naturally do whatever is necessary to get their way.

The Bible says that if parents don't confront those sinful tendencies, if they don't stand up to them, if they don't do everything in their power to expose them and to help children identify them and learn to control them internally, those sinful tendencies will eventually tyrannize the internal value systems of children and shipwreck their lives. The Bible warns us that if we don't discipline our children, we will ruin their lives.

SHARPENING THE FOCUS

Read Snapshot "Dealing with Discipline" before Question 4

Question Five Let me review some of the ABCs in the art of disciplining children. Although these notes will be brief, they will be helpful for you to review before leading your group. It might also be helpful to direct your group members to this section of the leader's notes for their own study.

Parents who really love their children had better be willing to express their love by becoming experts in the area of discipline. All *parents need to learn that they are capable of improving their discipline skills*. There are Christian books, tapes, film series, conferences, and seminars on this subject. These all explain in great detail the most effective, biblical ways to discipline children. Parents need to take advantage of them.

All parents need to learn how to *clearly communicate expectations* to their children. Explaining the rewards for compliance and the consequences for noncompliance is an essential. Once expectations are clearly communicated and understood, then comes the need for follow-through. Compliance brings rewards and noncompliance has to have its appropriate consequences. It is important that you are consistent in administering the consequences for noncompliance. You've got to follow through every single time.

You must also *discipline with discernment*. You shouldn't always discipline with military rigidity or at the other extreme—with a wink and a reprieve—but discipline with discernment. Did Michael break the rules intentionally and with malice? Did he decide with a defiant spirit to put his foot over the line to see if his parents would stand up to him? If that's what Michael is doing, his parents had better confront him. They better show him that limits are a part of life and that authority is for real.

However, it might have been that Michael just forgot the rule. Sometimes kids forget. Maybe there were extenuating circumstances that require special consideration and even a reduction in the severity of the consequences because it wasn't defiance at all. Maybe it was just absentmindedness. That might require a reminder and not discipline. The key is prayerful discernment in each situation.

Discernment determines when the best course of action for young children is a spanking, ten minutes on the time-out chair, or a warm, forgiving embrace that says, "I know you forgot, pal. I know you will do better next time." Discipline done with discernment determines when the best course of action for older children is having a restriction of privileges, extra chores, notes of apology, or acts of restitution. That discernment comes through study, reading, prayer, and conversation with other parents and developmental experts. It's every parent's responsibility to develop their personal discernment skills.

Another basic to constructive disciplining is to *make sure you follow up discipline with affirmations of love, warm embraces, and tender words*. You must explain to your children that you care for them so much that you cannot allow destructive attitudes and actions to undermine their lives and future. Some of the most tender moments I've had with my children have been after I've disciplined them firmly. I still carry memories of times with my daughter, Shauna, after I've disciplined her. I remember embracing her and saying, "Shauna, you're an incredible young lady. You matter to God. You're skilled and talented. You have a bright future in store for you. And I can't let you march into a bright future with the baggage you're carrying, because it won't serve you well. I had to do what I did because I love you, and I can't let those values and those behavioral patterns exist in your life." So many times she would wrap her arms around my neck and say, "Thanks, Dad. I love you, Dad."

We need to learn how to *finish the discipline process by saying, "Now it's over."* We've had our embraces, we've talked about it, and now we're done with it. Let's turn the page, start a new chapter, and move into the future with a close relationship.

Read Snapshot "Expressing Emotions" before Question 6

Questions Six & Seven I am thankful that there are caring Christian counselors and skilled therapists who have committed their lives to help emotionally wounded people heal. These counselors are saying, "Whatever you heard in your home, I'm here to say that your feelings matter. They mattered when you were young. They mattered when you were an adolescent. They mattered when you were in your twenties and thirties, and they matter now. So let's talk about it."

Christian counselors remind us that God has feelings. God experiences deep feelings. Read the Bible and you will see. He is never portrayed as a divine machine, an unaffected robo-god. He experiences delight and sorrow and anger and exasperation and great levels of joy. The Bible is very clear about God's expression of emotions.

When Jesus was on this earth He also expressed deep emotion: joy, sorrow, anger, and excitement were all part of Jesus' experience. Our feelings are an integral part of what makes us God's image bearers. Effective parenting demands that children's feelings be authenticated, affirmed, drawn out, and celebrated. They must also be discussed regularly so they can be interpreted carefully. We need to help our children learn to express positive and negative emotions constructively and not destructively.

Parents who learn how to shepherd the emotions of their children will be giving their kids a treasure that money can't buy. These parents give their children the right to experience feelings deeply and the skills to know how to express them appropriately. Do your kids feel free to talk about their emotions? Do you help them identify their feelings and communicate them?

Read Snapshot "Building Character" before Question 8

Question Eight I look back on some of the situations my dad pushed me into and the hard work he expected me to do, and now I understand that it was his way of giving me an opportunity to become strong. He could have made life easy for me, but he didn't. He insisted that I be put in situations where I would have an opportunity to become a mature adult. He wanted me to build character and a sense of responsibility.

Don't ever underestimate the importance of the first thirty years of Jesus' life as a carpenter. When I see movies portraying Jesus as a mystical, feminine, glassy-eyed weakling, I want to stand up and shout, "He was a tradesman for twenty years. He would have looked more like a construction worker than a pale, frail bookworm." I wonder how much strength, fortitude, courage, and perseverance was built into Jesus as His father Joseph had Him help haul logs, cut lumber, and work in the carpenter's shop. The challenge of working construction fourteen hours a day in the blistering Middle Eastern sun had to produce some character in Jesus. God didn't spare Him from hard work, splinters, and a sore back at the end of a hard day. The Father didn't bring Jesus into the world at thirty years old and say, "Now have a three-year ministry and come home." God gave His own Son challenges. In the same way, the challenges we place on our children will serve them well. We have to decide not to make the mistake of depriving our children from the very life experiences that can make them strong. Let's not overprovide or overprotect.

PUTTING YOURSELF IN THE PICTURE

Challenge group members to take time in the coming week to use part or all of this application section as an opportunity for continued growth.

THE HOME AS TRAUMA CENTER
GALATIANS 6:1—5

INTRODUCTION

We need to realize the critical importance of the home as a trauma center. Kids are getting emotionally beat up and shot at from every side. They need a safe place where they can experience healing and acceptance. If it does not happen in our homes, it will probably not happen anywhere.

Sometimes I wonder where family members go for treatment if the home is not functioning as a trauma center. Some husbands and dads go to bars and lounges to relax, wind down, and drink their troubles away. Some go on achievement binges, and others establish illicit relationships with people outside the family who offer a listening ear and a loving touch. Many moms and wives are doing the same thing these days. When young people find out that the family trauma center is closed, they turn to their peers who offer bad answers. Some actually hide their injuries for many, many years until those rather minor injuries get critically infected. None of these alternatives are God's best for family members. God's design is that every home function as a trauma center for every member of the family.

THE BIG PICTURE

Take time to read this introduction with the group. There are suggestions for how this can be done in the beginning of the leader's section.

A WIDE ANGLE VIEW

Question One I remember going to my study after my experience with Todd (described in the session introduction) to think over what had happened. I sat on the couch and thought, "I think I just had a close call in parenting. I think that was a self-esteem trauma for my son." I remember thinking, "I wonder what would have happened if I hadn't been around that night or if I hadn't stayed with him and given him a safe opportunity to tell me what was in his heart. I wonder how long he would have carried that burden alone. I wonder how many times he would have turned it over in his mind, "Oh, I'm weird am I? Maybe I am. Maybe I am." I remember thinking that night, "Boy, I almost feel like an emergency room doctor having just diagnosed an injury and applied treatment in the nick of time."

Then I thought, "I wonder how many of these nonmedical emergencies I've missed over the years. I wonder how many times my kids have experienced similar kinds of traumas that I never saw. I wonder how many of my direct family members have been wounded and received no treatment in my home? It was at that point that I asked God to help me think of my home as a trauma center for each of its members. A place where every family member can receive prompt, loving care for the everyday bumps, bruises, scrapes, and wounds of life. I hope you can begin to see your home as such a place.

A BIBLICAL PORTRAIT

Read Galatians 6:1–5

Question Three Remember Jesus' famous words in John 16:33? He said, "In this world you will have trouble." In other words, you need to expect trouble and plan on it. It is coming your way. Every member of every family is going to experience his or her share of pain. Every father and husband is going to have his setbacks, disappointments, marketplace embarrassments, and moral failures. The same could be said of every mother and every wife. Every child is going to experience some of the cruelty of life.

Rather than pretending this is not the case, we need to prepare our children to face a world that will sometimes break their hearts. If our homes become a place where we can bear burdens and bind up wounds, we will give our children a gift beyond measure.

SHARPENING THE FOCUS

Read Snapshot "A Qualified Staff" before Question 4

Question Four Educated parents would not tell their children that they should be seen and not heard. Rather, educated parents communicate that children are treasured. They are not an interruption. They are not an afterthought. Educated parents would never undercut the self-esteem of children by calling them stupid. Those words get seared into the consciousness of those defenseless little ones. They don't know how to interpret it. They just believe it. And they spend a lifetime trying to change the tape that plays in their mind.

Educated parents wouldn't force children to stuff emotions inside. Educated parents would do the exact opposite. They would teach their children how to express emotion. They would even go a step beyond this and learn to draw the emotions out of their children and train them to handle those emotions maturely and honestly. Educated parents wouldn't encourage children to put on false fronts before going out into public. Rather, educated parents would carefully train their children how to resolve conflict so that they don't have to go out with a mask on. This education does not usually happen in a formal class. It happens when we take parenting seriously. It happens when we begin asking the advice of parents we respect, when we begin to follow God's model of parenting, when we read good books and watch good videos. There are many helpful resources we can use.

There are more parenting materials and resources available to us than ever before in history. Bookshelves are sagging with the weight of excellent materials for the family. There are family videos, audiotapes, magazines, conferences, radio programs. All we have to do is commit ourselves to spending as much time reading family materials as we spend reading our magazines and newspapers. Maybe some evenings we need to turn off the TV and read a good book on parenting.

We have our children for only a season. During that season, determine to be a quality parent. Commit yourself to be a well-read, well-educated, well-informed, quality staff person in the trauma center unit in your home so that you are educated and equipped to train and treat your children properly during the brief time you have them.

Read Snapshot "Making Yourself Accessible" before Question 5

Question Six In Ephesians 6:4, Paul calls parents to not exasperate their children. Don't provoke them. Don't embitter them. Nothing exasperates a child like an absent parent. The mere absence causes bitterness.

Question: When and where in your family life can your kids say, "Dad, I have a problem" or "Mom, can I ask you something?" What are the office hours in your home trauma center? Where is the doctor's office? Where does this kind of thing young, bedtimes were fantastic opportunities for moments with children. I would like to challenge every father and mother with young children to make bedtime count. Go in and kneel down by the bed or lie on the bed and talk. Let them run off at the mouth a little. Sometimes during those moments, you stumble onto something that you can draw out and really talk about.

In addition to bedtime, take advantage of walks, bike rides, and meals alone as an opportunity to care for your children. Sometimes fathers and mothers need to get alone one-on-one with kids and ask them, "Is there anything that you would like to say to me now that we're alone and have plenty of time to talk?" We have to seize those moments because we don't get them back. When kids get older, their schedules start to fill up and social calendars bulge with activities. We need to spend time with them while we can.

Some families are experimenting with family night, an evening set aside for the whole family to be together once a week. I cheer you on. In our home we sometimes extend our dinner table discussions by making everybody have a mandatory cup of tea. It takes a little time for the water to boil, and then when the tea is ready, you have to sit there for a little while until it cools off. But it keeps us at the table for an extra twenty minutes. We need to be creative and create times for meaningful interaction and caring.

Read Snapshot "The Importance of Being Observant" before Question 7

Question Seven I have close friends who are in various lines of work. One of my friends is a car dealer. He can see a car going down the other side of a divided highway and say, "That car has been wrecked and repainted." I also have a friend who is a contractor. When we drive by a building, he can tell whether or not it was poorly designed. I marvel at these people. I wonder how many of us are that observant when it comes to our kids. How many of us scrutinize the attitudes, behavioral patterns, and conduct of our children so that we can make an early diagnosis of trouble that might be coming their way? This is a critical part of effective parenting.

PUTTING YOURSELF IN THE PICTURE

Challenge group members to take time in the coming week to use part or all of this application section as an opportunity for continued growth.

Teaching Faith in the Home

Deuteronomy 32:44–47

Introduction

The family can provide a kind of spiritual training that no other institution can match. A family has the potential to make deeper and longer lasting spiritual impressions on children than any other organization can. In the home children can receive ultimate, intensive, and comprehensive spiritual training if their parents are fully devoted followers of Christ.

What kind of specific marks are you going to try to make on your children? What are the basics truths that need to be impressed in the lives of children? What's the curriculum?

First, the essence of Christianity is a relationship. Second, serving Christ is the most satisfying activity or experience our children could ever have. And third, obeying the Lord leads to a blessed life. These are the core lessons all children should learn in the home.

The Big Picture

Take time to read this introduction with the group. There are suggestions for how this can be done in the beginning of the leader's section.

A Wide Angle View

Question One Another vivid spiritual memory I have comes from my junior high years. I was old enough to realize that my father was a successful businessman. I had hung around him enough at his place of employment to know he was very capable of playing hardball in the marketplace. But no matter how pressurized his life was and how much he traveled, he arranged everything so he could be home with the family on Sundays. We would all go to church together and then afterward, we would have Sunday dinner as a family. After our noon meal, my dad would drive all the way across town to the local mental hospital where he would lead a little devotional and song time for one hundred aging, forgotten, mentally retarded women. He led these services and ministered to these women for twenty-five years.

Every once in a while he would ask one of us children to go with him. Sometimes we would even volunteer. I remember that one of these services fell on a Christmas Sunday. I was hoping my dad wouldn't make me go, because I wanted to play with my new toys. Out of all the kids he could have invited, he said, "Billy, come on. Let's go." He had the trunk of his car filled with gifts. We dragged them in and he held his little song time with those women. It was the only service they would attend. After the service, he pulled those boxes to the back of the chapel and as the women came out from that chapel, I watched my dad greet every one of them by name. He embraced many of them. I watched my dad wrap his arms around these unattractive, unkempt, aging, retarded women. "Oh Francis, Merry Christmas. I found something for you. Helen, oh Helen, Merry Christmas." One by one they filed out, and one by one he showed them the love of Jesus. I remember looking into his eyes as he was looking into the eyes of those women, and I saw a love that could only come from God.

A Biblical Portrait

Read Deuteronomy 32:44–47

Question Two Many parents have tried a number of different ways to delegate the spiritual training of their children to others. They send them to Sunday school, Christian school, youth group, catechism classes, confirmation classes, and the like. All of these things might be good and profitable, but they don't reflect the central place of spiritual learning for children. The bottom line is that the central and primary place for spiritual growth in the lives of children is in the home, and the primary teachers are parents.

We dads and moms tend to parent children enthusiastically in our areas of personal competence. If a mother happens to be a trained musician, it's not uncommon for children to be taking piano lessons early in life. If a father is an avid athlete, he puts a little barbell set in the corner of the crib and says, "C'mon, get with it, pal. Let's pump iron. Hurry and grow up so that we can do athletic things together." We tend to parent enthusiastically in the area of our own competence.

Here's where things get messy. Many parents don't feel all that competent in the area of their spiritual lives. Those of us who have walked with the Lord for many years are painfully aware of our sins and our spiritual failures. This can lead to a parental inferiority complex in the area of providing spiritual training for our kids. So we decide to delegate the responsibility to someone else. We need to be reminded that whatever the church or other organizations or individuals offer our kids, these things must be viewed as supplemental. God knows exactly what He is doing by laying this responsibility squarely on the shoulders of parents.

There is great wisdom in God's strategy at this point. The fact is, parents who sincerely attempt to teach and train their children spiritually will end up growing more than their children. The teacher always learns more than the student. Part of God's wisdom in giving parents the role of the primary spiritual trainers of their children is God's desire to grow up parents and not just grow up kids. No matter how old your children are, you're still their spiritual trainer.

SHARPENING THE FOCUS

Read Snapshot "A Dynamic Relationship with God" before Question 3

Question Four As parents, our example is critically important. We can model a legalistic faith that is about rules and regulations or a joyous and dynamic relationship with the living God. Our model and example will make all the difference in the world. Allow time for your group members to honestly identify some of the ways parents model the wrong message. Also, encourage them to discuss practical ways they can help their children understand what faith is really about.

Read Snapshot "Serving God" before Question 5

Questions Five & Six I remember talking with a Christian father in his midfifties over a cup of coffee. He broke down in tears telling me about his thirty-five-year-old son who was still chasing every experience, toy, award, and thrill. And he said, "Every time I see that boy, a pain shoots through my heart, because he's squandering his life looking for satisfaction that only Christ can give."

I want to teach my own kids what Jesus said over and over again: If you really want to find fulfillment in this life, you find it by giving your life away to His service and to the service of others. If you want to gain life, Jesus said, lose it in service to God and others. I want to teach my kids that they will never find ultimate satisfaction through self-gratification. They will only find what they are looking for, in terms of real fulfillment, through serving God and giving themselves away to others.

My dad had a sailboat, an airplane, and lots of other toys, but I never saw a greater satisfaction in his eyes than when he led worship for those women at the Kalamazoo mental hospital. He was most alive when he was serving God. We need to help our children learn these same valuable lessons early in life.

Read Snapshot "Rich Rewards" before Question 7

Questions Seven & Eight When Jesus was on this earth, He took a handful of untrained fishermen and He said to them the two most powerful words that a spiritual teacher can say to a spiritual learner: "Follow me." "Walk with me, talk with me, watch me, ask me questions, challenge me if you want, but follow me." And in three short years, the handful of leaders that Jesus started with had been transformed into a group of men so strong spiritually that they turned the world upside down. They changed the course of human history. Jesus' classroom was the world. His lecture was His life. He left unforgettable spiritual marks on His followers. And parents, the methodology Jesus used has never been outdated. The two most powerful words you can say to your children in your attempt to mark them spiritually are "Follow me."

If you want your kids to learn that Christianity is about a living relationship with Jesus, then make sure you model that kind of relationship. If you relate to God in a genuine way, it would be difficult for your kids to arrive at any other conclusion. If you want your kids to serve God and find satisfaction in doing so, then discover your spiritual gift and use it for God's glory. Serve enthusiastically and just let your kids see the satisfaction you have found in living for Christ. If you want your kids to obey God, then you obey God, and let them observe the blessedness that comes from leading an obedient life.

Putting Yourself in the Picture

Challenge group members to take time in the coming week to use part or all of this application section as an opportunity for continued growth.

ADDITIONAL WILLOW CREEK RESOURCES

Small Group Resources

Coaching Life-Changing Small Group Leaders, by Bill Donahue and Greg Bowman
The Complete Book of Questions, by Garry Poole
The Connecting Church, by Randy Frazee
Leading Life-Changing Small Groups, by Bill Donahue and the Willow Creek Team
The Seven Deadly Sins of Small Group Ministry, by Bill Donahue and Russ Robinson
Walking the Small Group Tightrope, by Bill Donahue and Russ Robinson

Evangelism Resources

Becoming a Contagious Christian (book), by Bill Hybels and Mark Mittelberg
The Case for a Creator, by Lee Strobel
The Case for Christ, by Lee Strobel
The Case for Faith, by Lee Strobel
Seeker Small Groups, by Garry Poole
The Three Habits of Highly Contagious Christians, by Garry Poole

Spiritual Gifts and Ministry

Network Revised (training course), by Bruce Bugbee and Don Cousins
The Volunteer Revolution, by Bill Hybels
What You Do Best in the Body of Christ—Revised, by Bruce Bugbee

Marriage and Parenting

Fit to Be Tied, by Bill and Lynne Hybels
Surviving a Spiritual Mismatch in Marriage, by Lee and Leslie Strobel

Ministry Resources

An Hour on Sunday, by Nancy Beach
Building a Church of Small Groups, by Bill Donahue and Russ Robinson
The Heart of the Artist, by Rory Noland
Making Your Children's Ministry the Best Hour of Every Kid's Week, by Sue Miller and David Staal
Thriving as an Artist in the Church, by Rory Noland

Curriculum

An Ordinary Day with Jesus, by John Ortberg and Ruth Haley Barton
Becoming a Contagious Christian (kit), by Mark Mittelberg, Lee Strobel, and Bill Hybels
Good Sense Budget Course, by Dick Towner, John Tofilon, and the Willow Creek Team
If You Want to Walk on Water, You've Got to Get Out of the Boat, by John Ortberg with Stephen and Amanda Sorenson
The Life You've Always Wanted, by John Ortberg with Stephen and Amanda Sorenson
The Old Testament Challenge, by John Ortberg with Kevin and Sherry Harney, Mindy Caliguire, and Judson Poling

WILLOW
Willow Creek Association

Willow Creek Association
Vision, Training, Resources for Prevailing Churches

This resource was created to serve you and to help you build a local church that prevails. It is just one of many ministry tools that are part of the Willow Creek Resources® line, published by the Willow Creek Association together with Zondervan.

The Willow Creek Association (WCA) was created in 1992 to serve a rapidly growing number of churches from across the denominational spectrum that are committed to helping unchurched people become fully devoted followers of Christ. Membership in the WCA now numbers over 10,500 Member Churches worldwide from more than ninety denominations.

The Willow Creek Association links like-minded Christian leaders with each other and with strategic vision, training, and resources in order to help them build prevailing churches designed to reach their redemptive potential. Here are some of the ways the WCA does that.

- **A2: Building Prevailing Acts 2 Churches—Today**—an annual two-and-a-half day event, held at Willow Creek Community Church in South Barrington, Illinois, to explore strategies for building churches that reach out to seekers and build believers, and to discover new innovations and breakthroughs from Acts 2 churches around the country.

- **The Leadership Summit**—a once a year, two-and-a-half-day conference to envision and equip Christians with leadership gifts and responsibilities. Presented live at Willow Creek as well as via satellite broadcast to over one hundred locations across North America, this event is designed to increase the leadership effectiveness of pastors, ministry staff, volunteer church leaders, and Christians in the marketplace.

- **Ministry-Specific Conferences**—throughout each year the WCA hosts a variety of conferences and training events—both at Willow Creek's main campus and offsite, across the U.S., and around the world—targeting church leaders and volunteers in ministry-specific areas such as: evangelism, small groups, preaching and teaching, the arts, children, students, women, volunteers, stewardship, raising up resources, etc.

- **Willow Creek Resources®**—provides churches with trusted and field-tested ministry resources in such areas as leadership, evangelism, spiritual formation, spiritual gifts, small groups, stewardship, student ministry, children's ministry, the use of the arts-drama, media, contemporary music —and more.

- **WCA Member Benefits**—includes substantial discounts to WCA training events, a 20 percent discount on all Willow Creek Resources®, *Defining Moments* monthly audio journal for leaders, quarterly *Willow* magazine, access to a Members-Only section on WillowNet, monthly communications, and more. Member Churches also receive special discounts and premier services through WCA's growing number of ministry partners—Select Service Providers—and save an average of $500 annually depending on the level of engagement.

For specific information about WCA conferences, resources, membership, and other ministry services contact:

Willow Creek Association
P.O. Box 3188
Barrington, IL 60011-3188
Phone: 847-570-9812
Fax: 847-765-5046
www.willowcreek.com

Continue building your new community!
New Community Series
BILL HYBELS AND JOHN ORTBERG
with Kevin and Sherry Harney

Exodus: *Journey Toward God* 0-310-22771-2

Parables: *Imagine Life God's Way* 0-310-22881-6

Sermon on the Mount[1]: *Connect with God* 0-310-22884-0

Sermon on the Mount[2]: *Connect with Others* 0-310-22883-2

Acts: *Build Community* 0-310-22770-4

Romans: *Find Freedom* 0-310-22765-8

Philippians: *Run the Race* 0-310-22766-6

Colossians: *Discover the New You* 0-310-22769-0

James: *Live Wisely* 0-310-22767-4

1 Peter: *Stand Strong* 0-310-22773-9

1 John: *Love Each Other* 0-310-22768-2

Revelation: *Experience God's Power* 0-310-22882-4

Look for New Community at your local Christian bookstore.

Continue the Transformation
Pursuing Spiritual Transformation
JOHN ORTBERG, LAURIE PEDERSON,
AND JUDSON POLING

Grace: *An Invitation to a Way of Life* 0-310-22074-2

Growth: *Training vs. Trying* 0-310-22075-0

Groups: *The Life-Giving Power of Community* 0-310-22076-9

Gifts: *The Joy of Serving God* 0-310-22077-7

Giving: *Unlocking the Heart of Good Stewardship* 0-310-22078-5

Fully Devoted: *Living Each Day in Jesus' Name* 0-310-22073-4

Look for Pursuing Spiritual Transformation at your local Christian bookstore.

TOUGH QUESTIONS
Garry Poole and Judson Poling

Softcover

How Does Anyone Know God Exists?	ISBN 0-310-24502-8
What Difference Does Jesus Make?	ISBN 0-310-24503-6
How Reliable Is the Bible?	ISBN 0-310-24504-4
How Could God Allow Suffering and Evil?	ISBN 0-310-24505-2
Don't All Religions Lead to God?	ISBN 0-310-24506-0
Do Science and the Bible Conflict?	ISBN 0-310-24507-9
Why Become a Christian?	ISBN 0-310-24508-7
Leader's Guide	ISBN 0-310-24509-5

REALITY CHECK SERIES
by Mark Ashton

Winning at Life	ISBN: 0-310-24525-7
Leadership Jesus Style	ISBN: 0-310-24526-5
When Tragedy Strikes	ISBN: 0-310-24524-9
Sudden Impact	ISBN: 0-310-24522-2
Jesus' Greatest Moments	ISBN: 0-310-24528-1
Hot Issues	ISBN: 0-310-24523-0
Future Shock	ISBN: 0-310-24527-3
Clear Evidence	ISBN: 0-310-24746-2

We want to hear from you. Please send your comments about this book to us in care of zreview@zondervan.com. Thank you.

GRAND RAPIDS, MICHIGAN 49530 USA

WWW.ZONDERVAN.COM